My

GRATITUDE

JOURNAL

My Information

1. What is your absolute favorite aspect of your routine?
2. What is the food you love most?
3. Write about your most loved music.
4. What do you enjoy the most about your home.
5. Five things that you are proud of.
6. Which person are you the most grateful about in life?
7. Record a moment when someone impressed you with manners or kindness.
8. What are you most fond of in your appearance?
9. What's your favourite trees or plants?
10. Tell us about your most favorite outfit.
11. What is your favorite spot at home?
12. What are the benefits that you can get from your work?
13. Three things that you admire about yourself.
14. What is your most-loved food?
15. What family member or persons do you feel most grateful to?
16. Give us a list of hobbies you are passionate about.
17. What is it that makes you feel relaxed and calm?
18. What is it that makes you laugh?
19. Recall your most memorable memories from your childhood.
20. What are your top memories from high school?
21. Grown-up memories?

22. Write about the most memorable day you've ever experienced.

23. What is it that makes you feel rich?

24. Write about what you're great at.

25. How can you assist others?

26. What kind of books, videos or other media have you recently enjoyed?

27. What are the top presents you've received?

28. Tell us about a time when you were happy with yourself for having made an excellent decision.

29. What are the things you're grateful for that to not find in the world?

30. What life lessons have acquired that you'd like be able to

31.Are there any things you can accept and be thankful for the lessons you have learned?

32. List a few times when you've lucked out.

33. Make a list of the best choices you've made.

34. What romantic relationships are you thankful for both in the current and past?

35. Choose the top destinations you've visited.

36. Who do you feel most grateful to meet in your life?

37. What can technology do to improve your life?

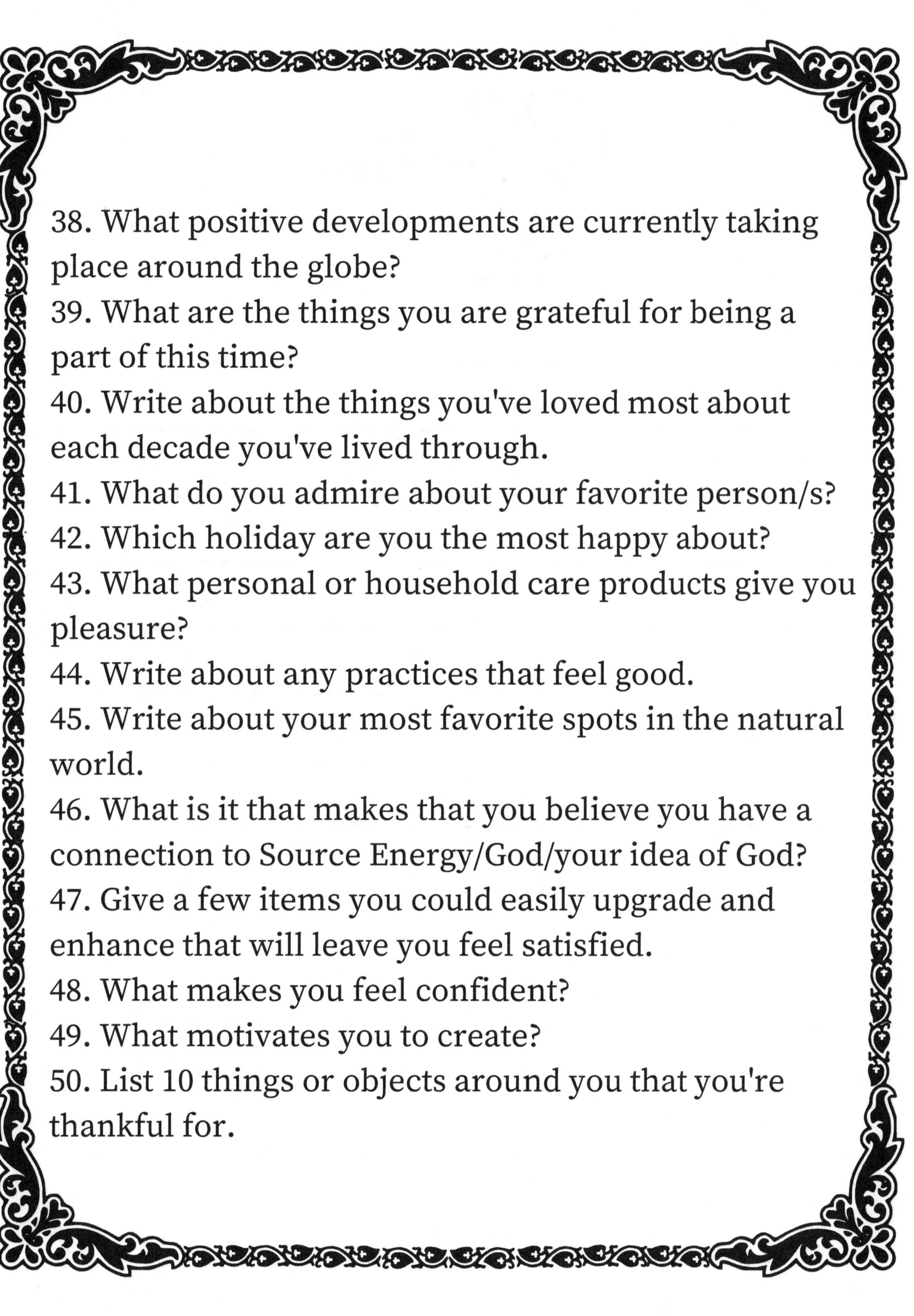

38. What positive developments are currently taking place around the globe?

39. What are the things you are grateful for being a part of this time?

40. Write about the things you've loved most about each decade you've lived through.

41. What do you admire about your favorite person/s?

42. Which holiday are you the most happy about?

43. What personal or household care products give you pleasure?

44. Write about any practices that feel good.

45. Write about your most favorite spots in the natural world.

46. What is it that makes that you believe you have a connection to Source Energy/God/your idea of God?

47. Give a few items you could easily upgrade and enhance that will leave you feel satisfied.

48. What makes you feel confident?

49. What motivates you to create?

50. List 10 things or objects around you that you're thankful for.

Notes

My Favorite Activities Which Make Me Happy:

I'll Try to Make Them More Often through:

Why I Love My Life

Places I love To Visit

____

____

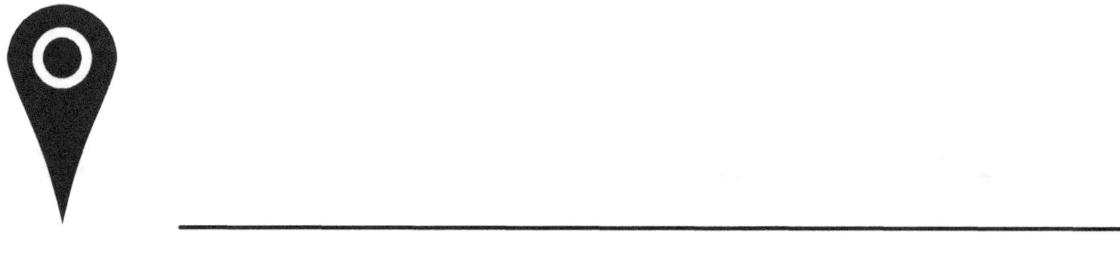

____

____

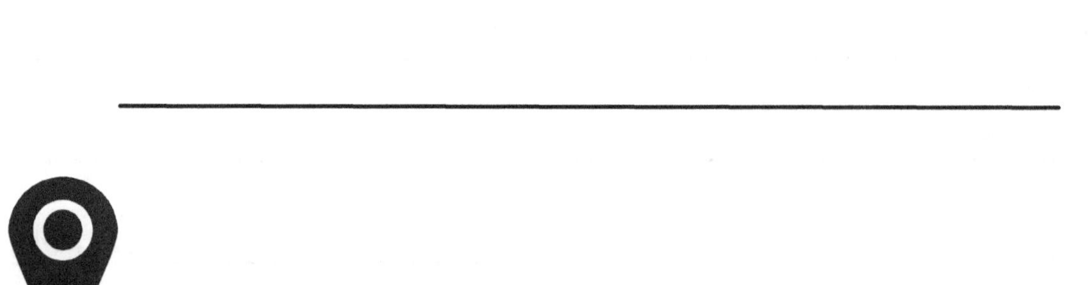

____

People
I am Grateful For

BOOKS
I am Grateful For

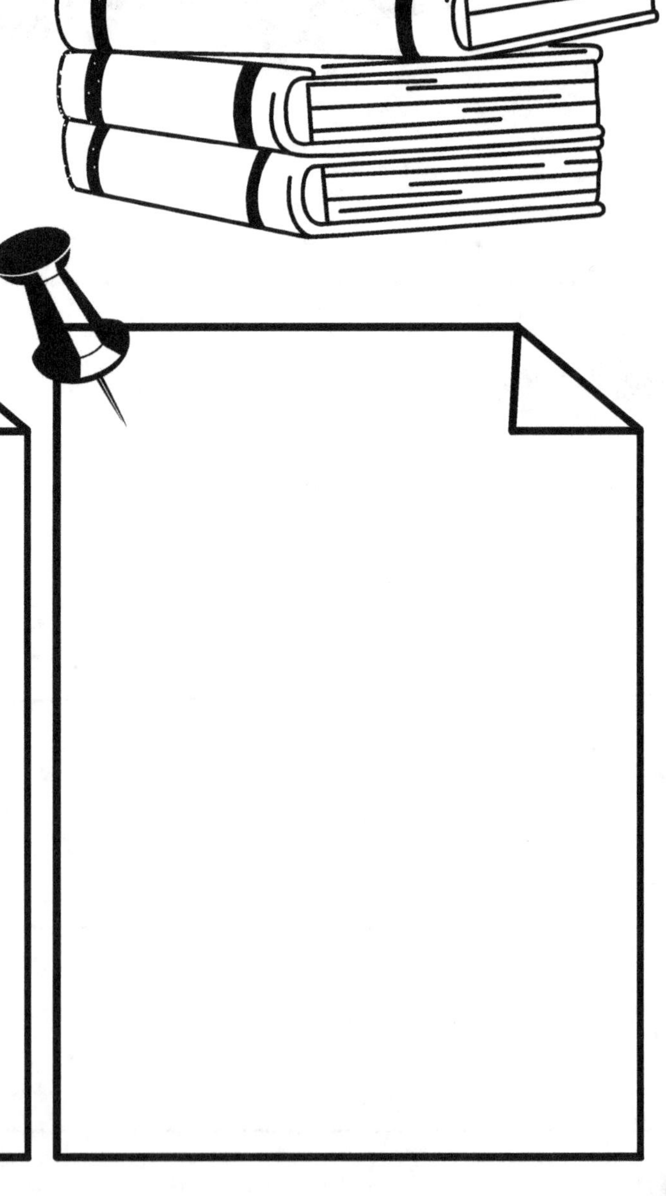

TV SHOWS
I Enjoyed Most

Dear
THANK YOU

Grateful For :
Monday
Tuesday
Wednesday

Thursday
Friday
Saturday
Sunday

Notes

My Favorite Activities Which Make Me Happy:

I'll Try to Make Them More Often through:

Why I Love My Life

Places I love To Visit

People
I am Grateful For

BOOKS
I am Grateful For

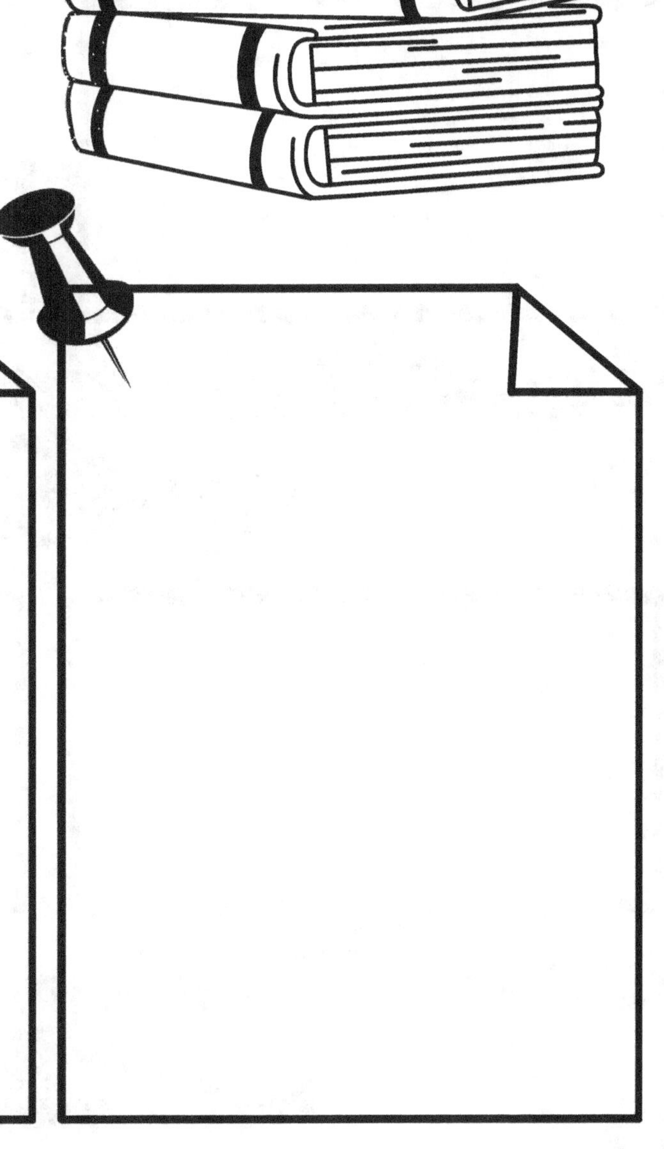

TV SHOWS
I Enjoyed Most

Dear ....

Grateful For :
Monday
Tuesday
Wednesday

Thursday

Friday

Saturday

Sunday

Notes

Date:

My Favorite Activities Which Make Me Happy:

I'll Try to Make Them More Often through:

Why I Love My Life

Places I love To Visit

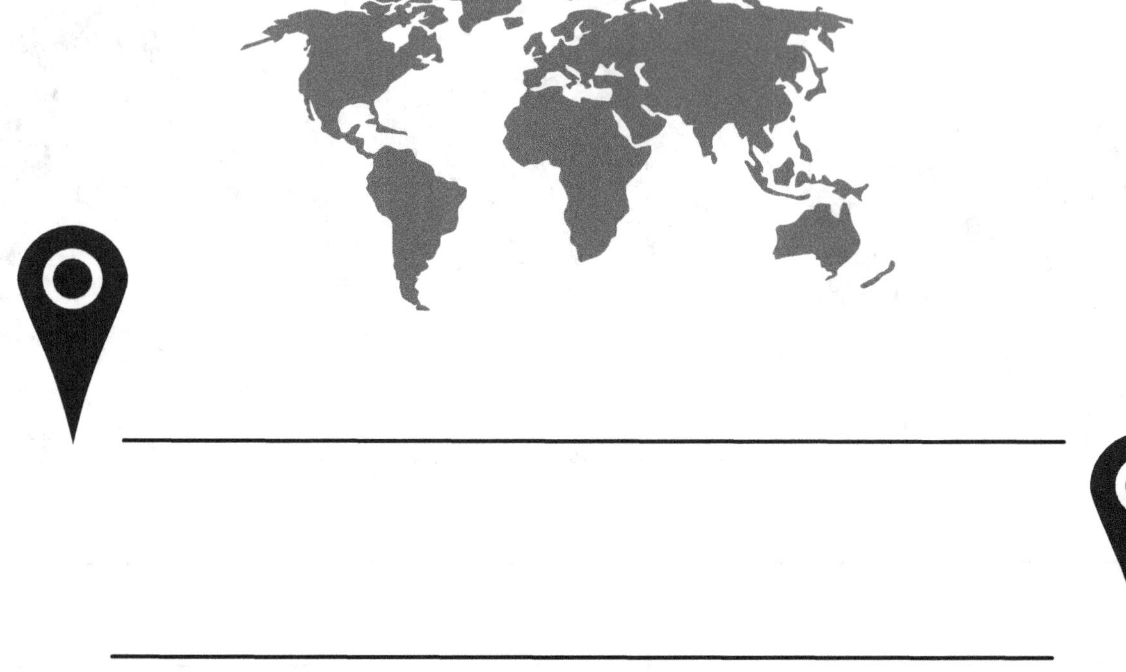

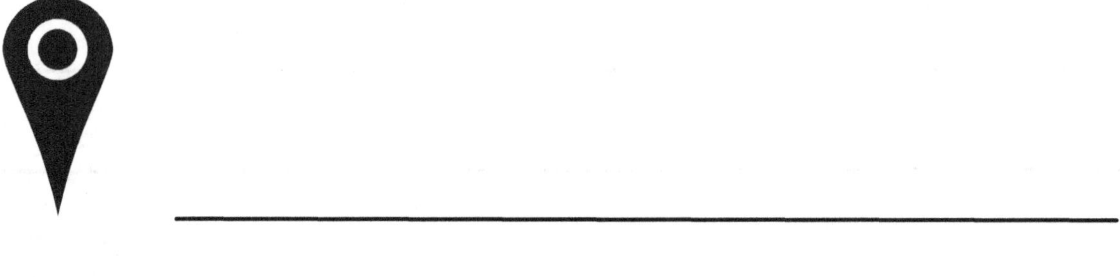

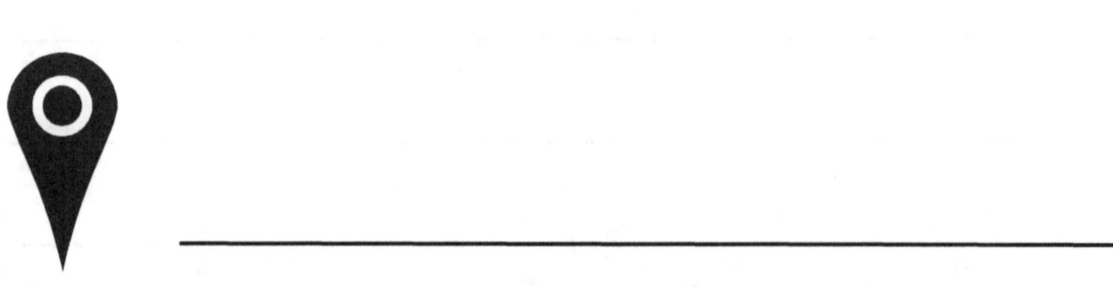

People I am Grateful For

BOOKS
I am Grateful For

TV SHOWS
I Enjoyed Most

Dear ....

Grateful For :

Monday

Tuesday

Wednesday

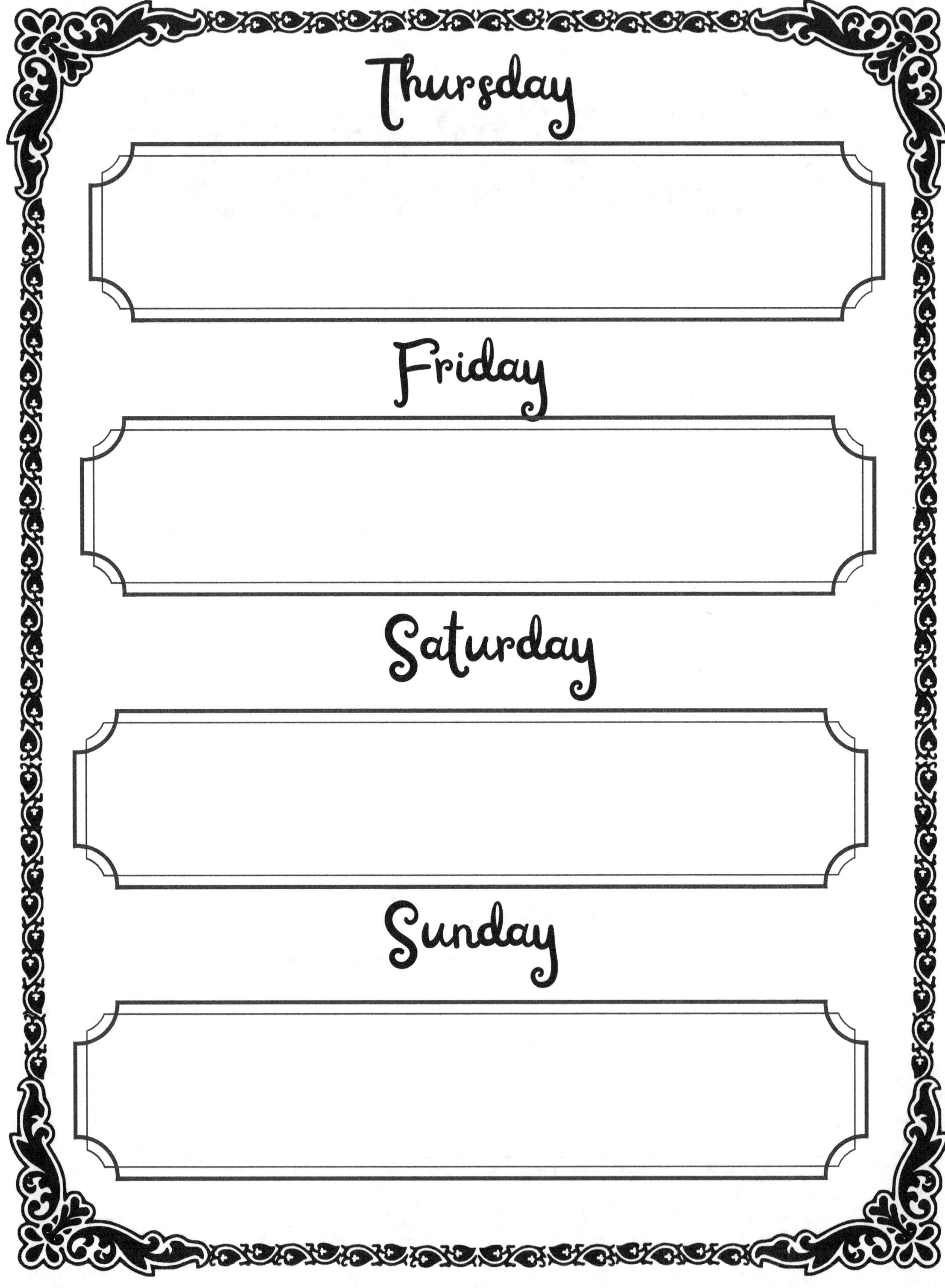
Thursday
Friday
Saturday
Sunday

Notes

My Favorite Activities Which Make Me Happy:

____

____

____

____

____

I'll Try to Make Them More Often through:

____

____

____

____

____

Why I Love My Life

Places I love To Visit

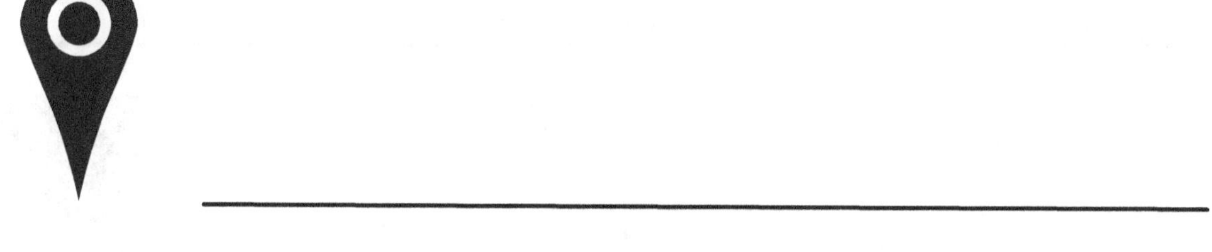

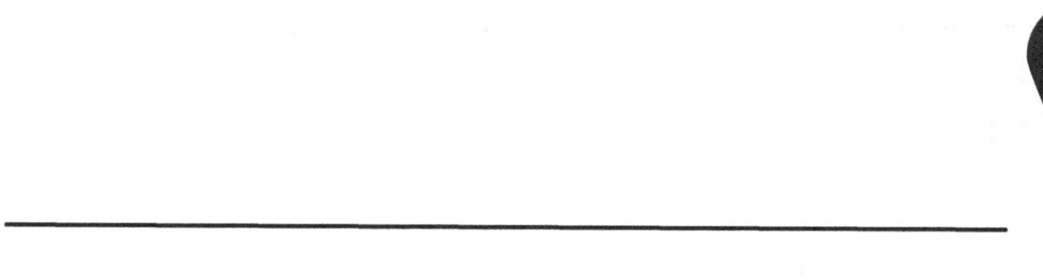

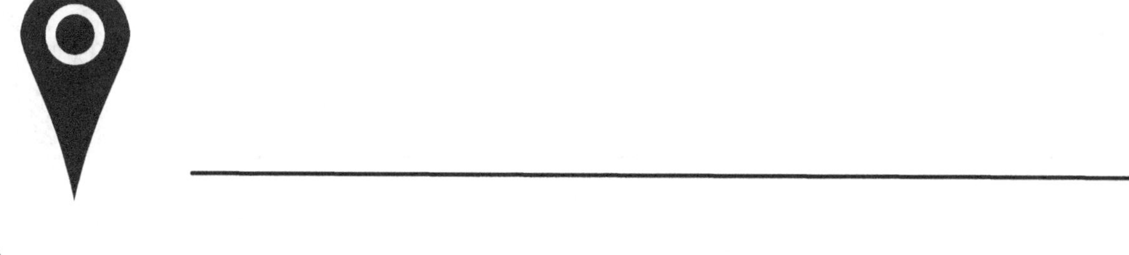

People
I am Grateful For

BOOKS
I am Grateful For

TV SHOWS

I Enjoyed Most

Dear ....

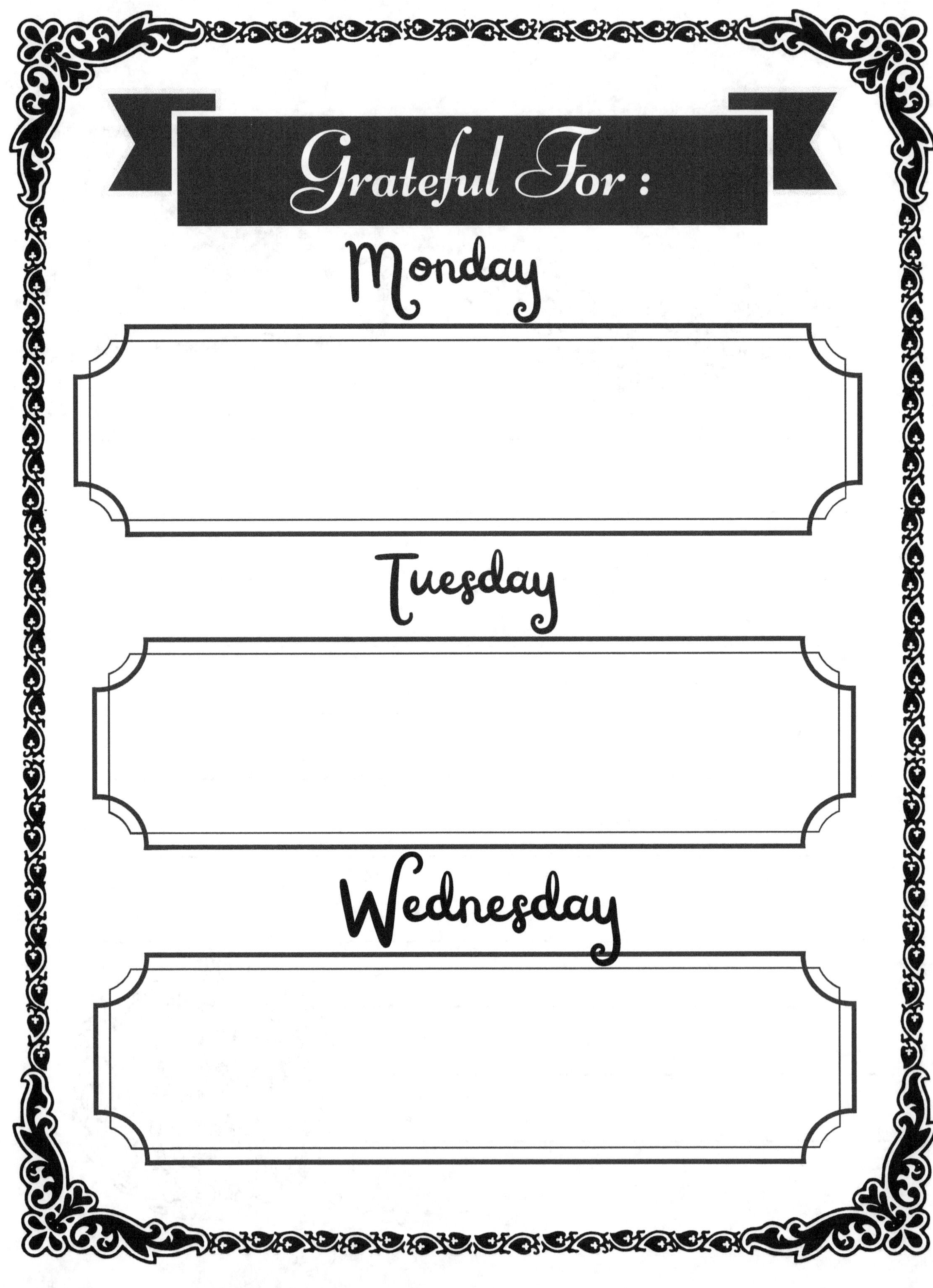
Grateful For :
Monday
Tuesday
Wednesday

Thursday
Friday
Saturday
Sunday

Notes

My Favorite Activities Which Make Me Happy:

I'll Try to Make Them More Often through:

Why I Love My Life

Places I love To Visit

People I am Grateful For

BOOKS

I am Grateful For

GOOD BOOKS
&
GOOD COMPANY

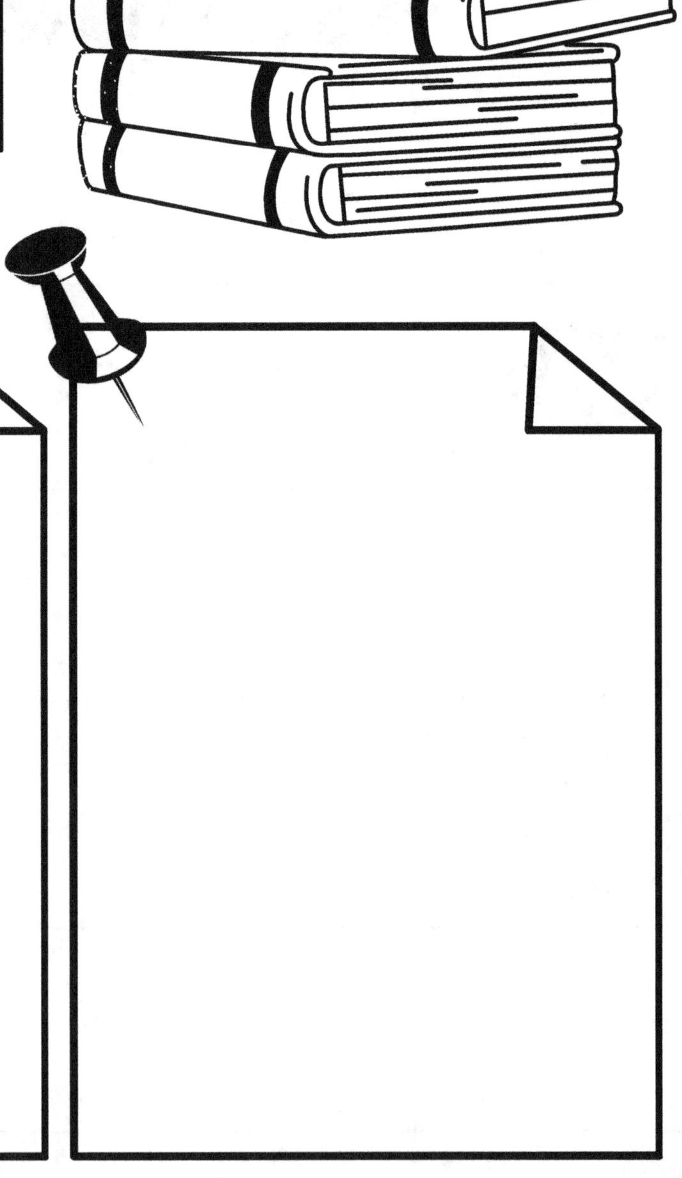

TV SHOWS

I Enjoyed Most

Dear
THANK YOU

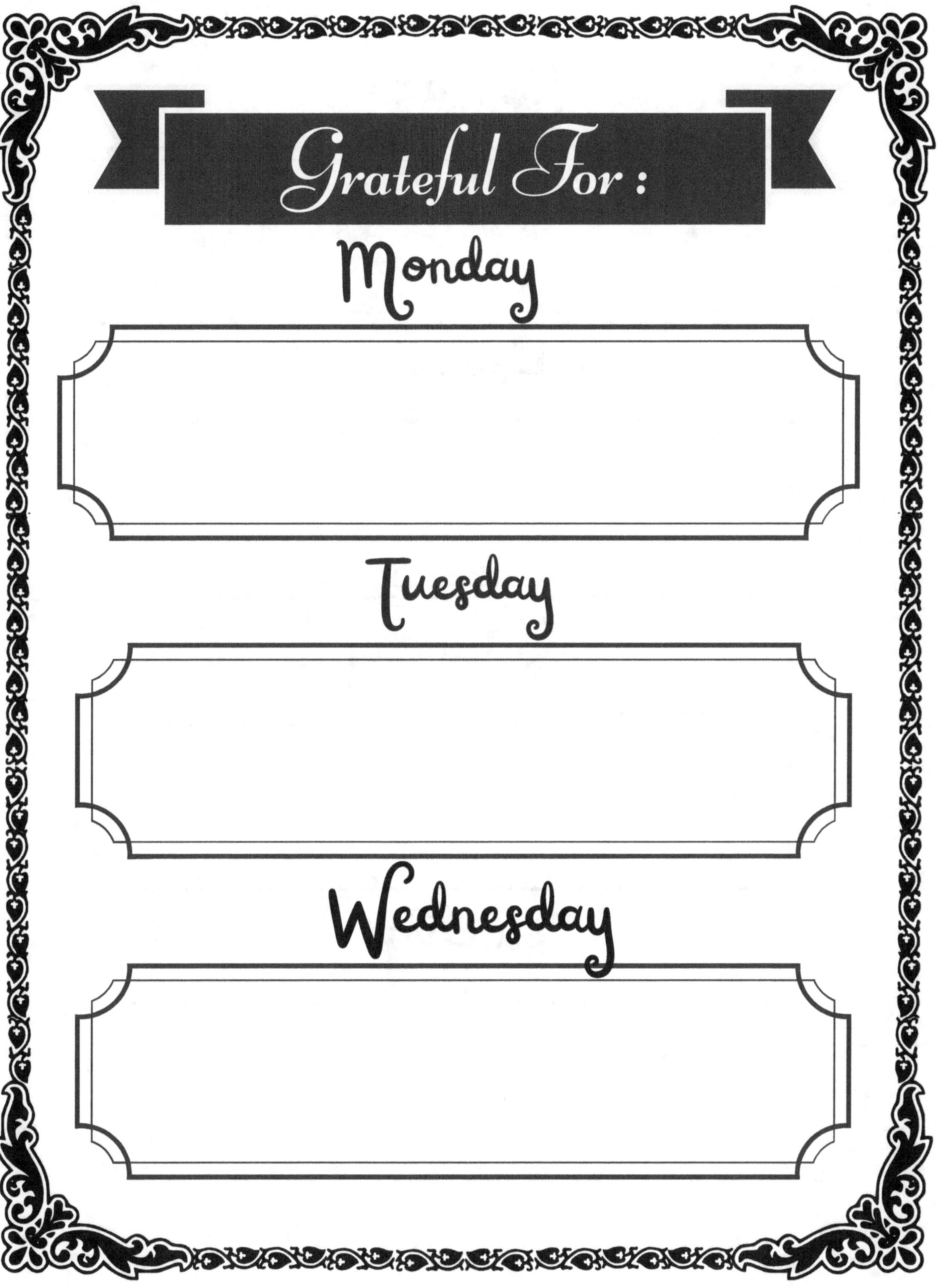

Grateful For :
Monday
Tuesday
Wednesday

Thursday
Friday
Saturday
Sunday

Notes

My Favorite Activities Which Make Me Happy:

I'll Try to Make Them More Often through:

Why I Love My Life

Places I love To Visit

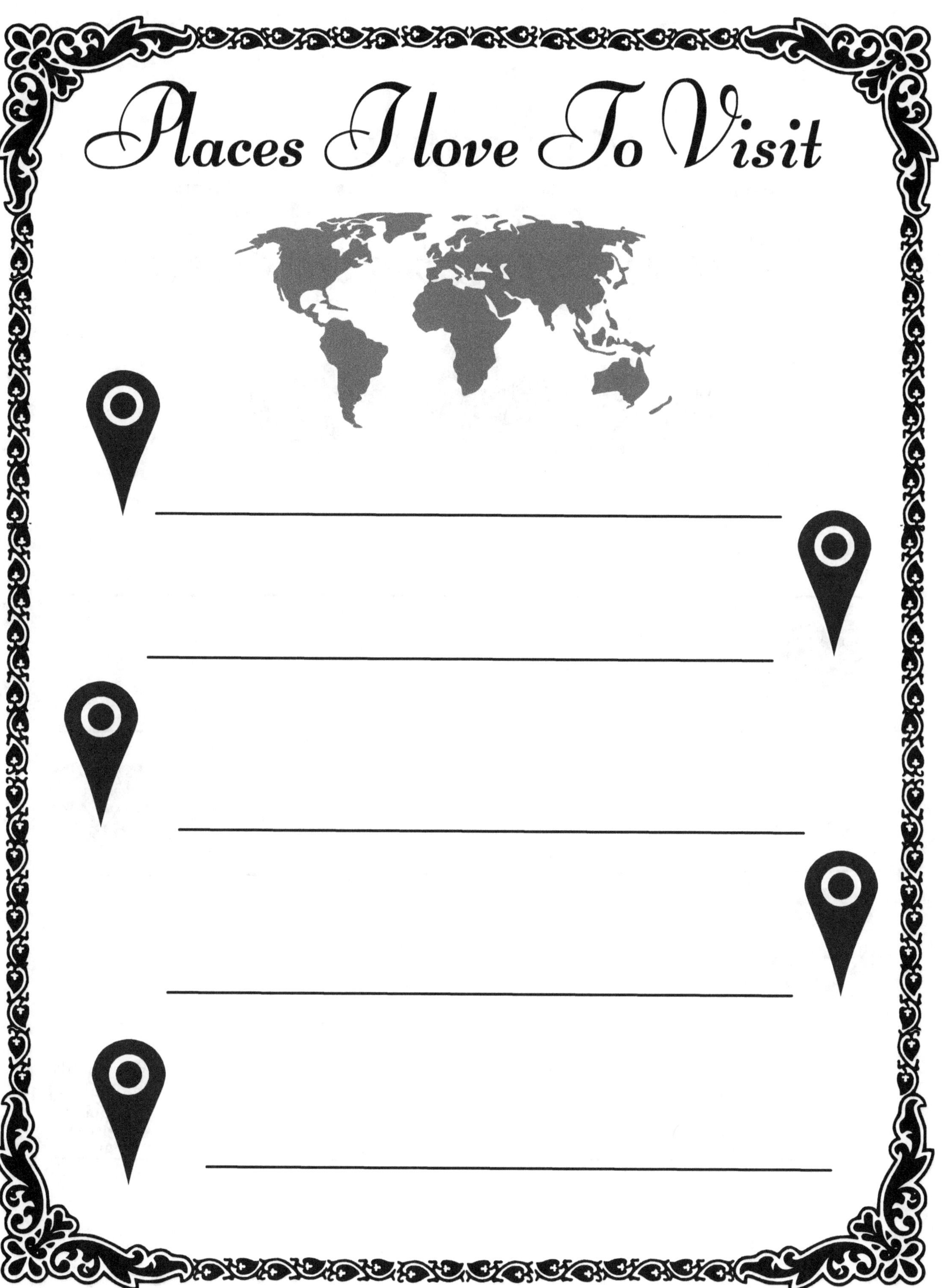

People I am Grateful For

BOOKS

I am Grateful For

TV SHOWS

I Enjoyed Most

Dear ....

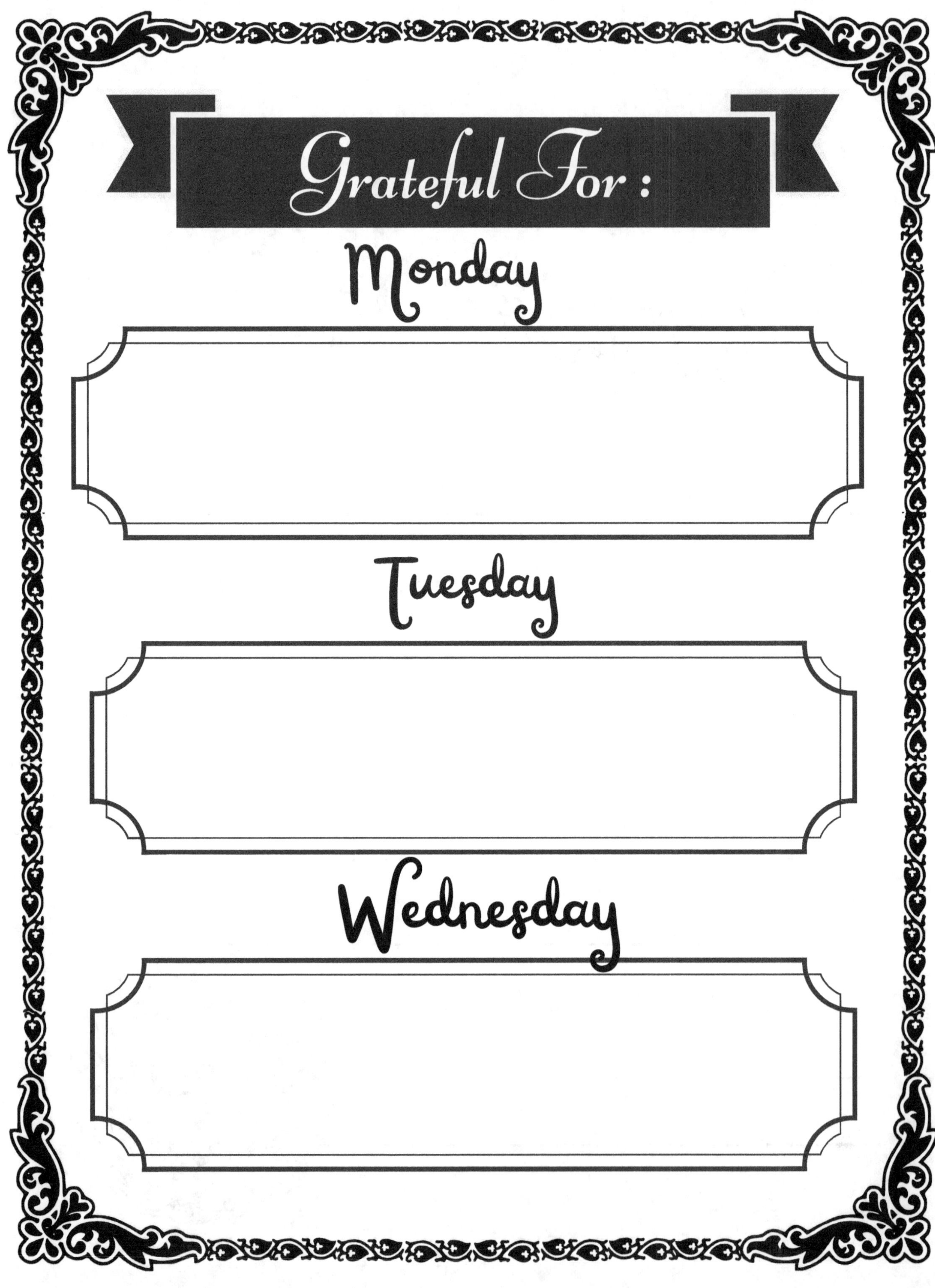
Grateful For :
Monday
Tuesday
Wednesday

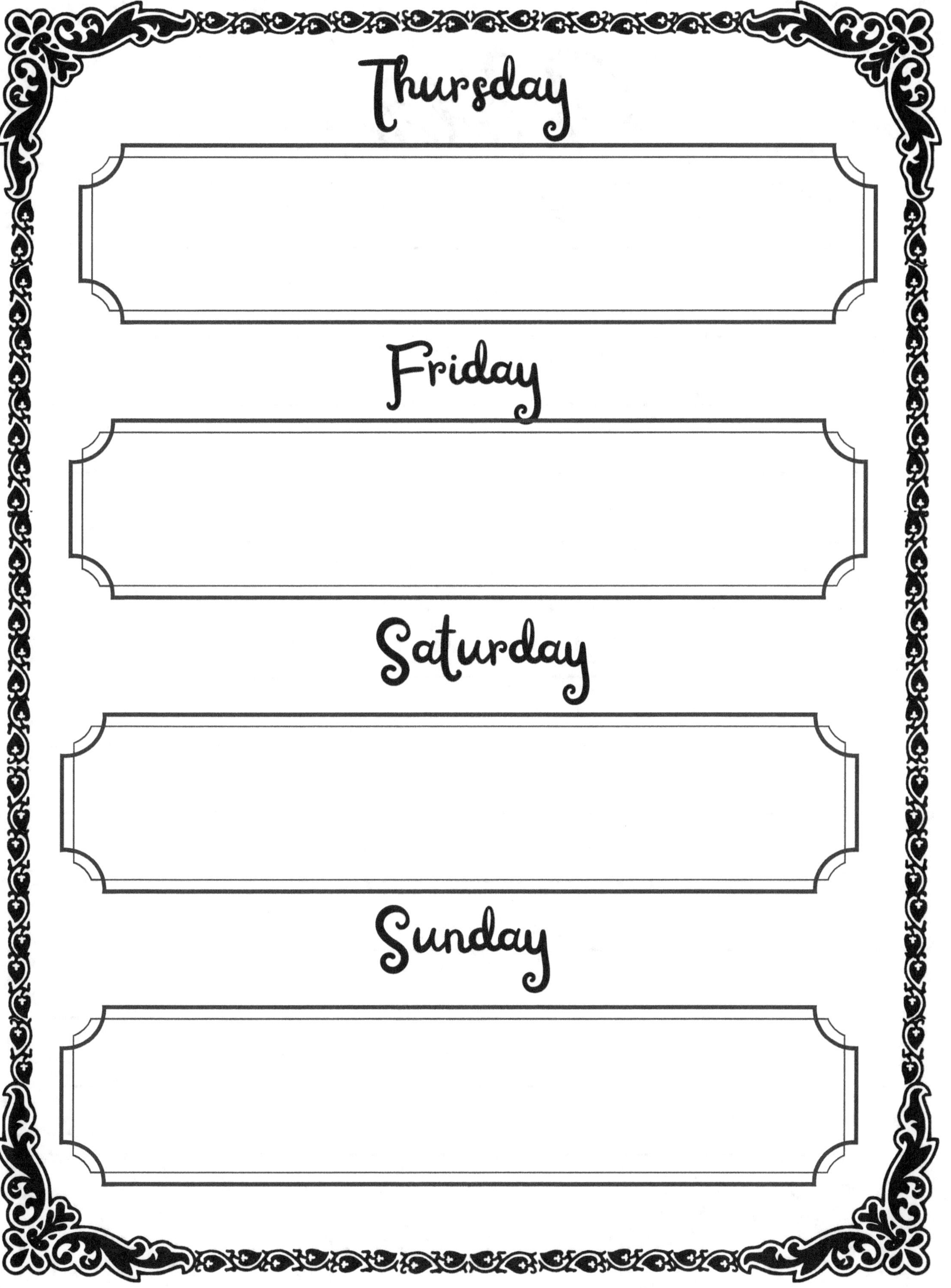

Thursday
Friday
Saturday
Sunday

Notes

My Favorite Activities Which Make Me Happy:

I'll Try to Make Them More Often through:

Why I Love My Life

Places I love To Visit

People
I am Grateful For

BOOKS

I am Grateful For

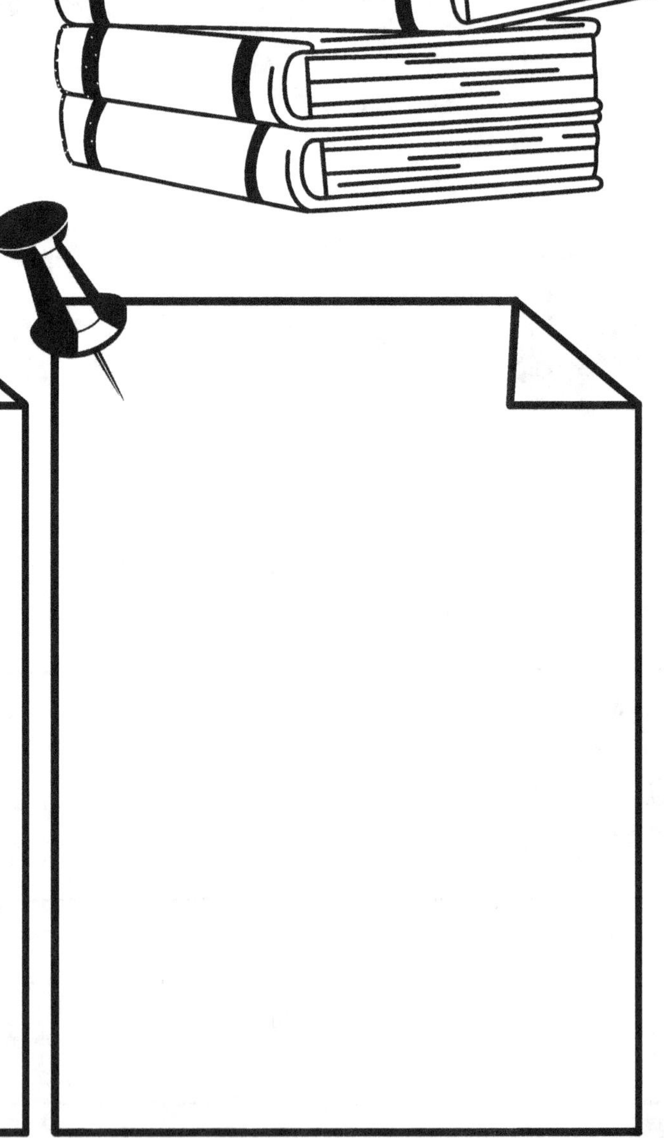

TV SHOWS
I Enjoyed Most

Dear ....

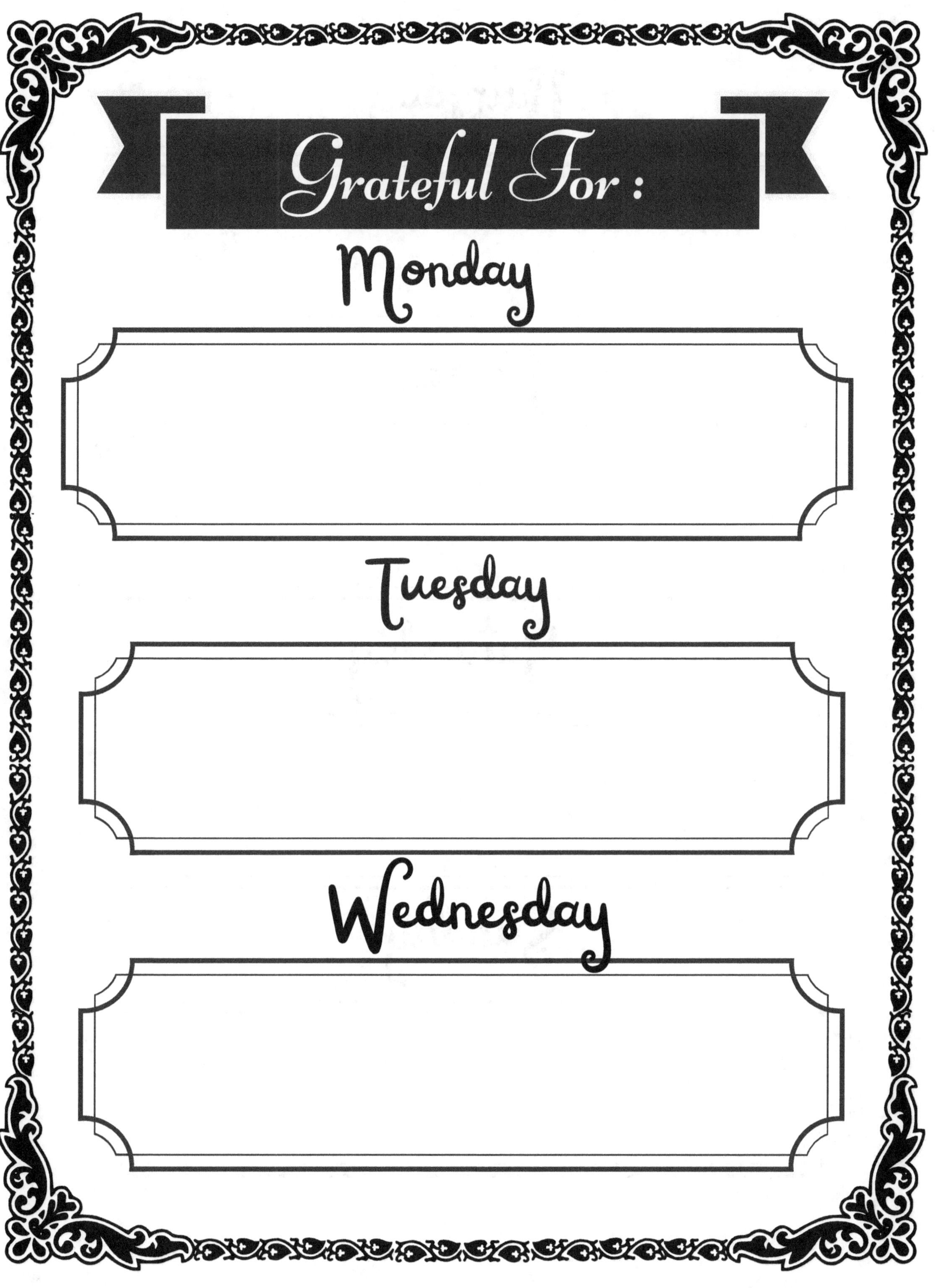

Grateful For :
Monday
Tuesday
Wednesday

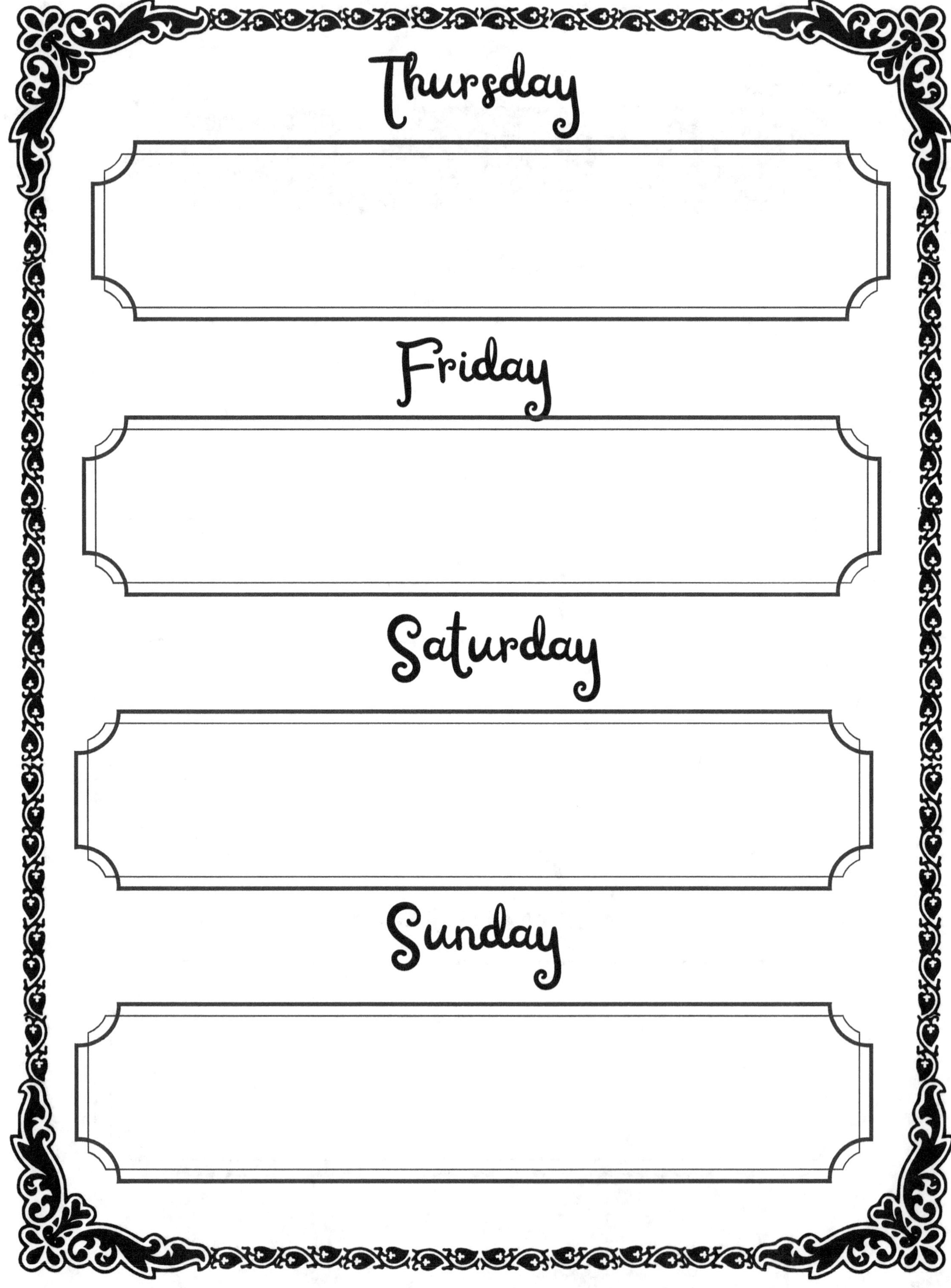

Thursday
Friday
Saturday
Sunday

Notes

My Favorite Activities Which Make Me Happy:

I'll Try to Make Them More Often through:

Why I Love My Life

Places I love To Visit

People I am Grateful For

BOOKS
I am Grateful For

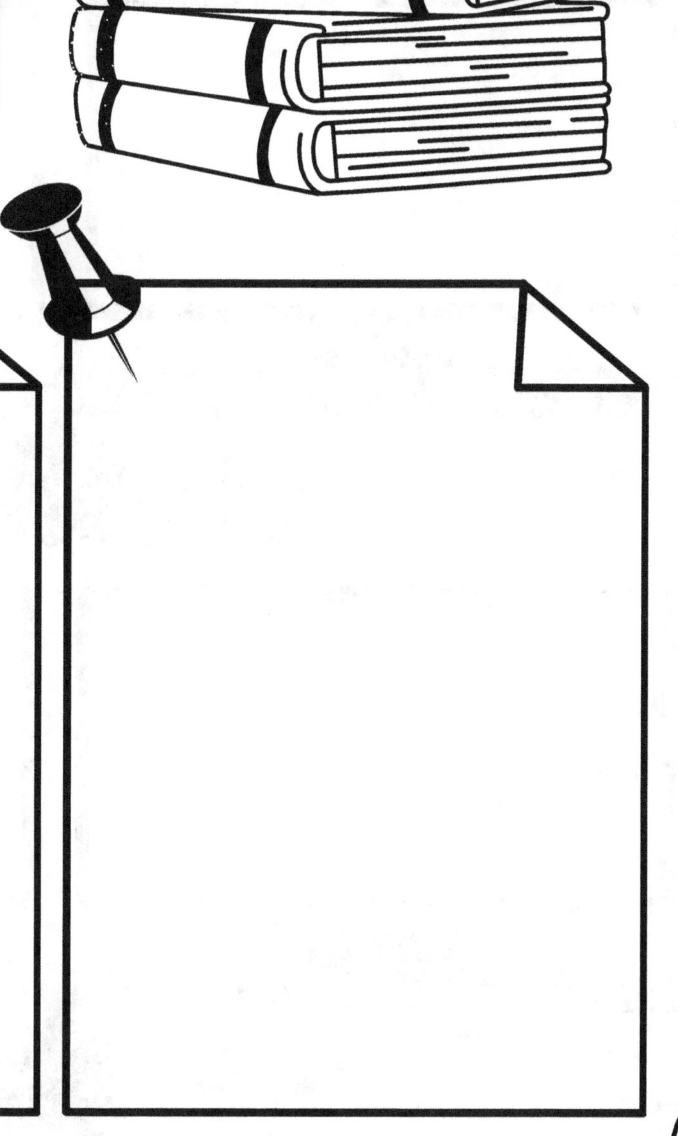

TV SHOWS

I Enjoyed Most

Dear
THANK YOU

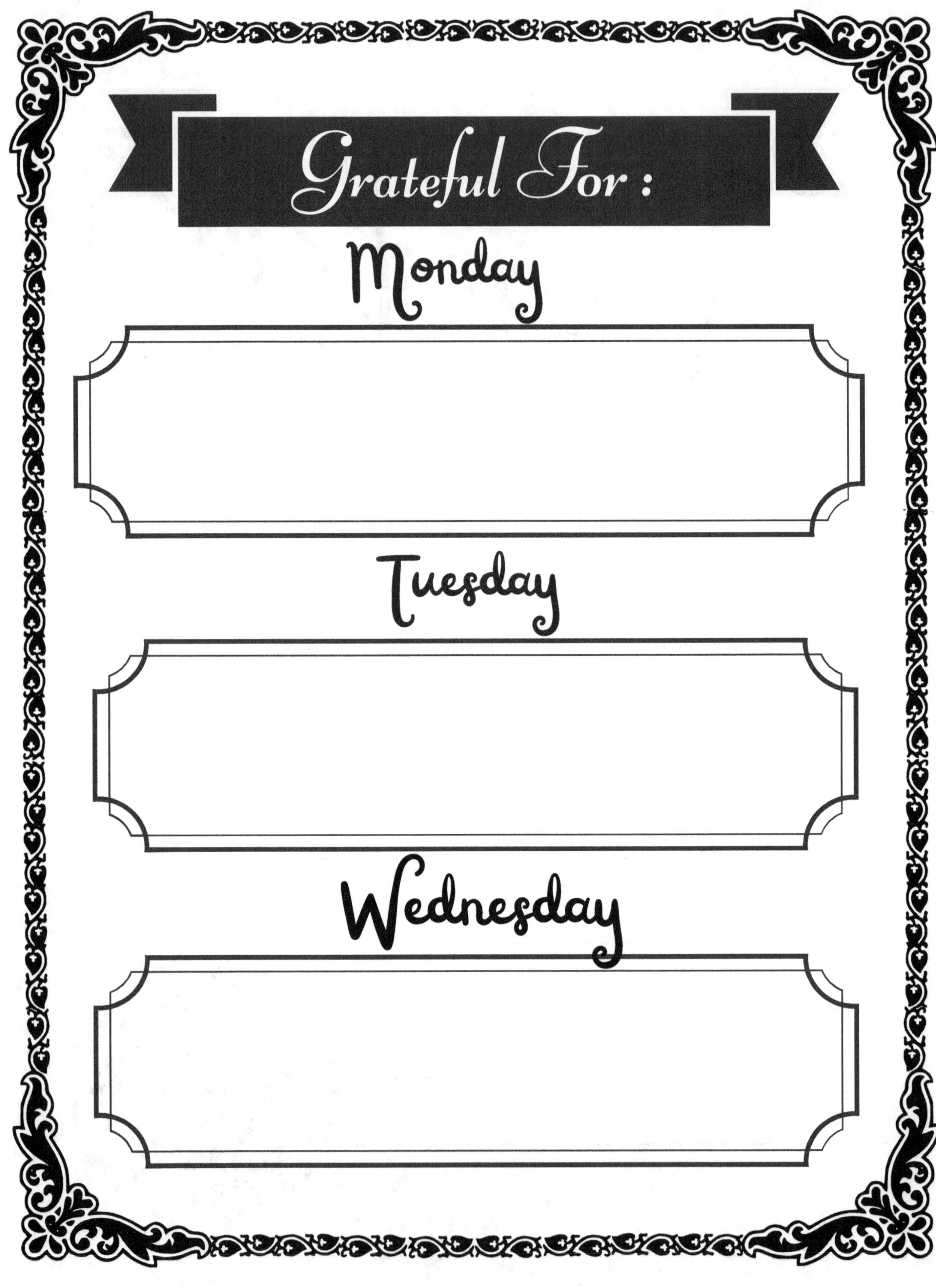
Grateful For :
Monday
Tuesday
Wednesday

# Thursday

Friday

Saturday

Sunday

Notes

Date:

My Favorite Activities Which Make
Me Happy:

I'll Try to Make Them More
Often through:

Why I Love My Life

Places I love To Visit

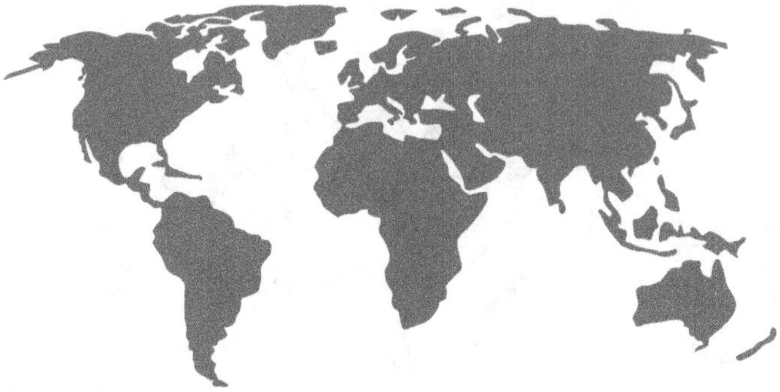

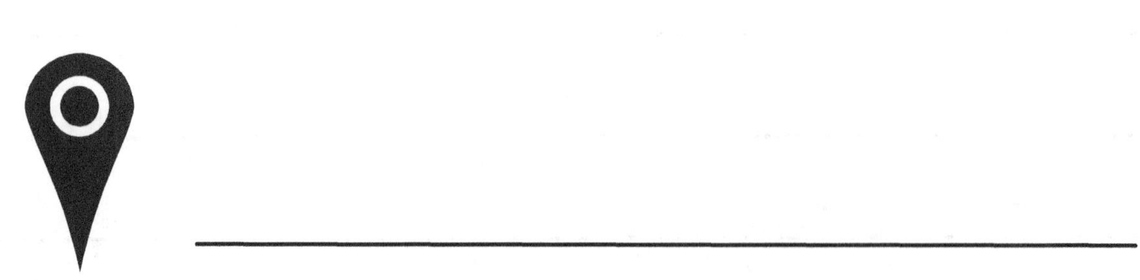

People
I am Grateful For

BOOKS

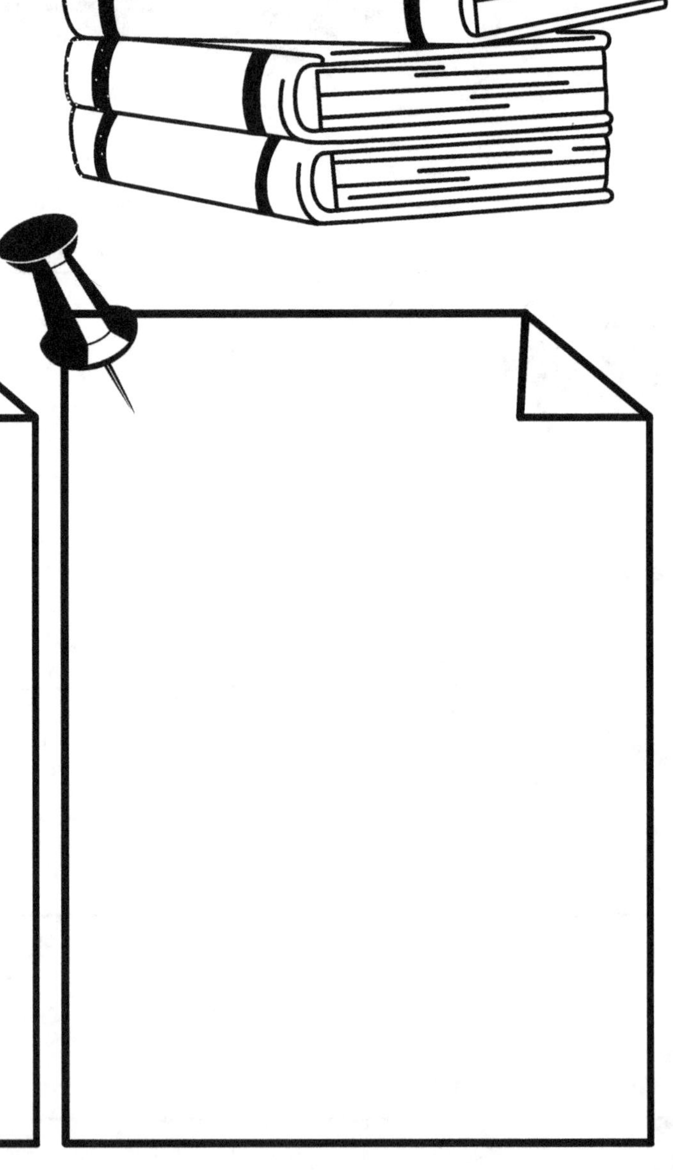

TV SHOWS
I Enjoyed Most

Dear
THANK YOU

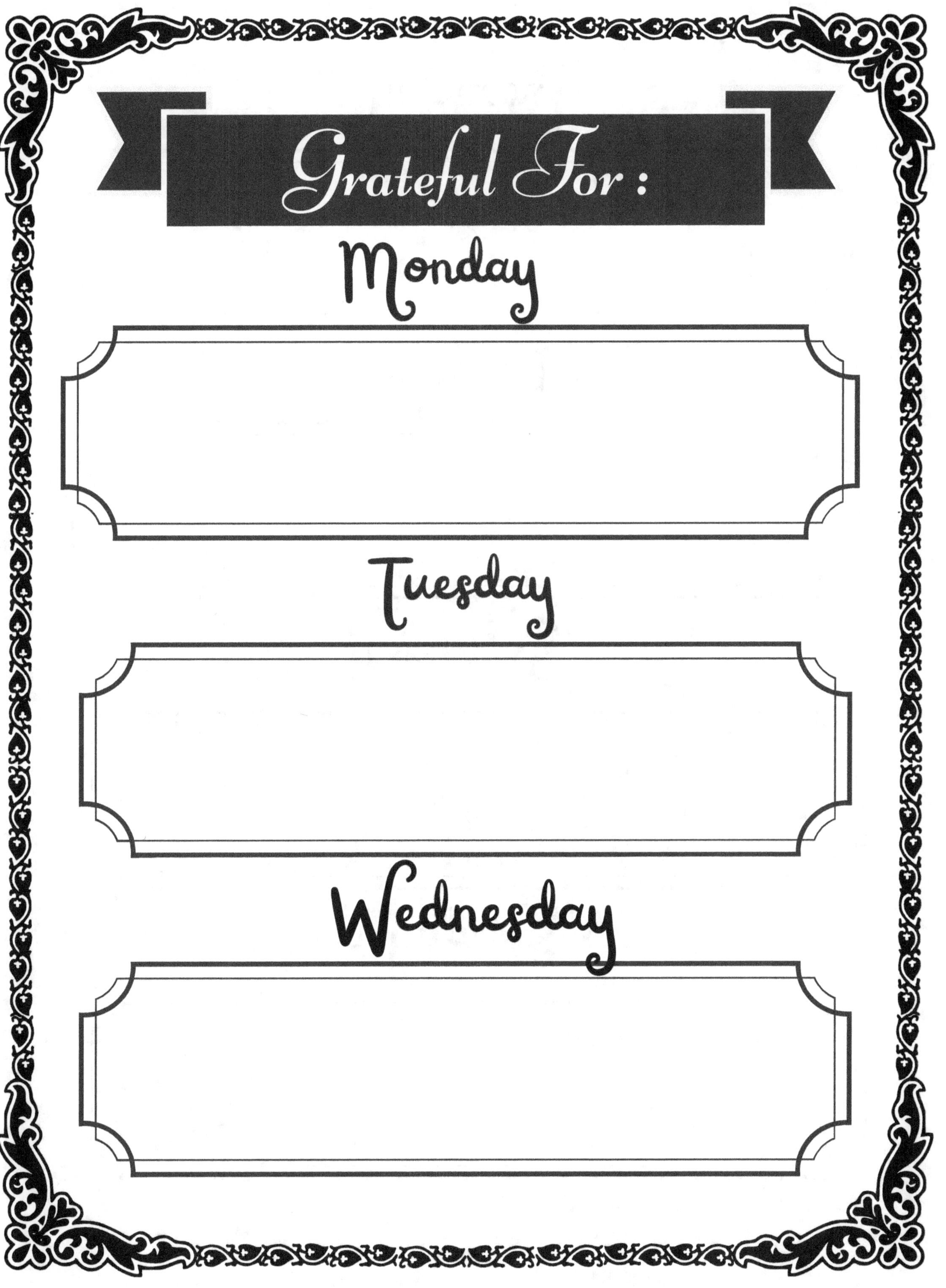
Grateful For :
Monday
Tuesday
Wednesday

Thursday

Friday

Saturday

Sunday

Notes

Date:

My Favorite Activities Which Make Me Happy:

I'll Try to Make Them More Often through:

Why I Love My Life

Places I love To Visit

People
I am Grateful For

BOOKS

I am Grateful For

GOOD BOOKS
&
GOOD COMPANY

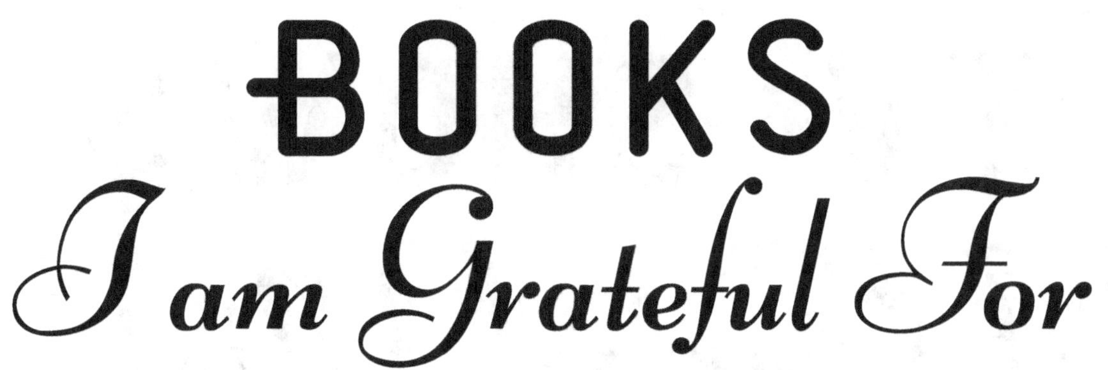

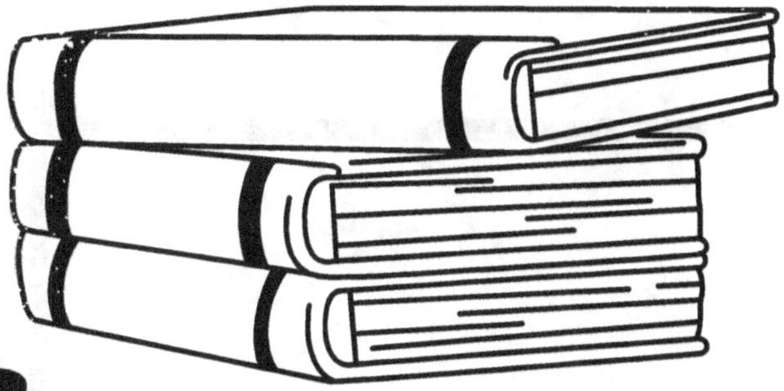

TV SHOWS
I Enjoyed Most

Dear

Grateful For :
Monday
Tuesday
Wednesday

Thursday
Friday
Saturday
Sunday

Notes
Date:

My Favorite Activities Which Make Me Happy:

I'll Try to Make Them More Often through:

Why I Love My Life

Places I love To Visit

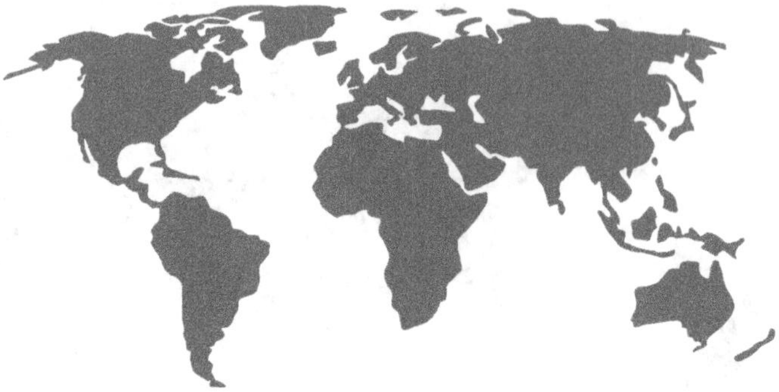

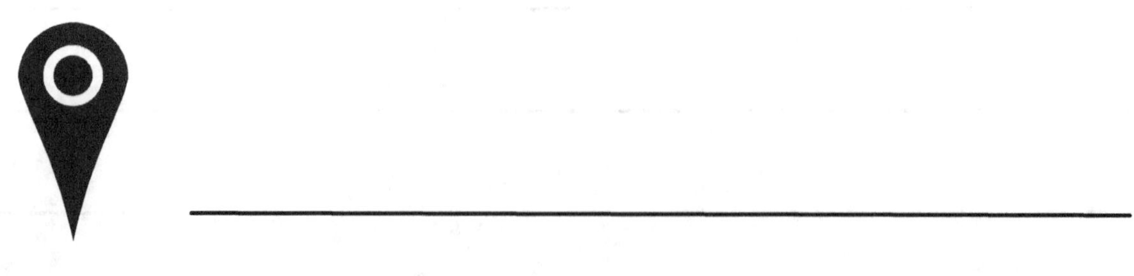

People
I am Grateful For

BOOKS
I am Grateful For

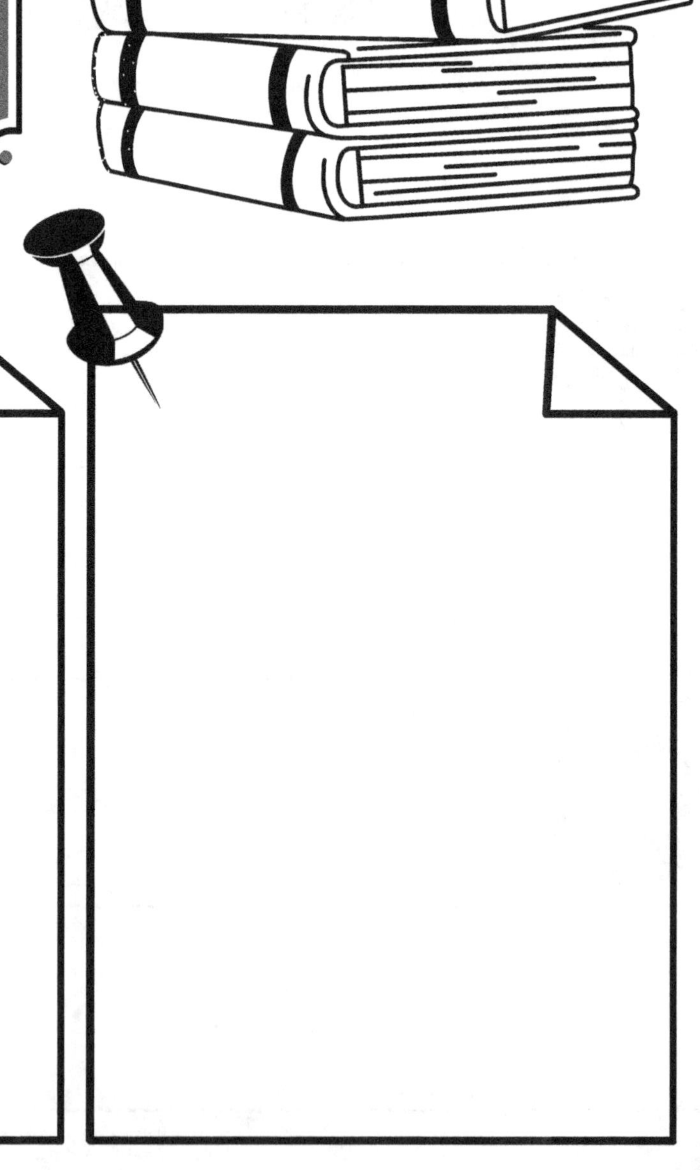

TV SHOWS

I Enjoyed Most

Dear

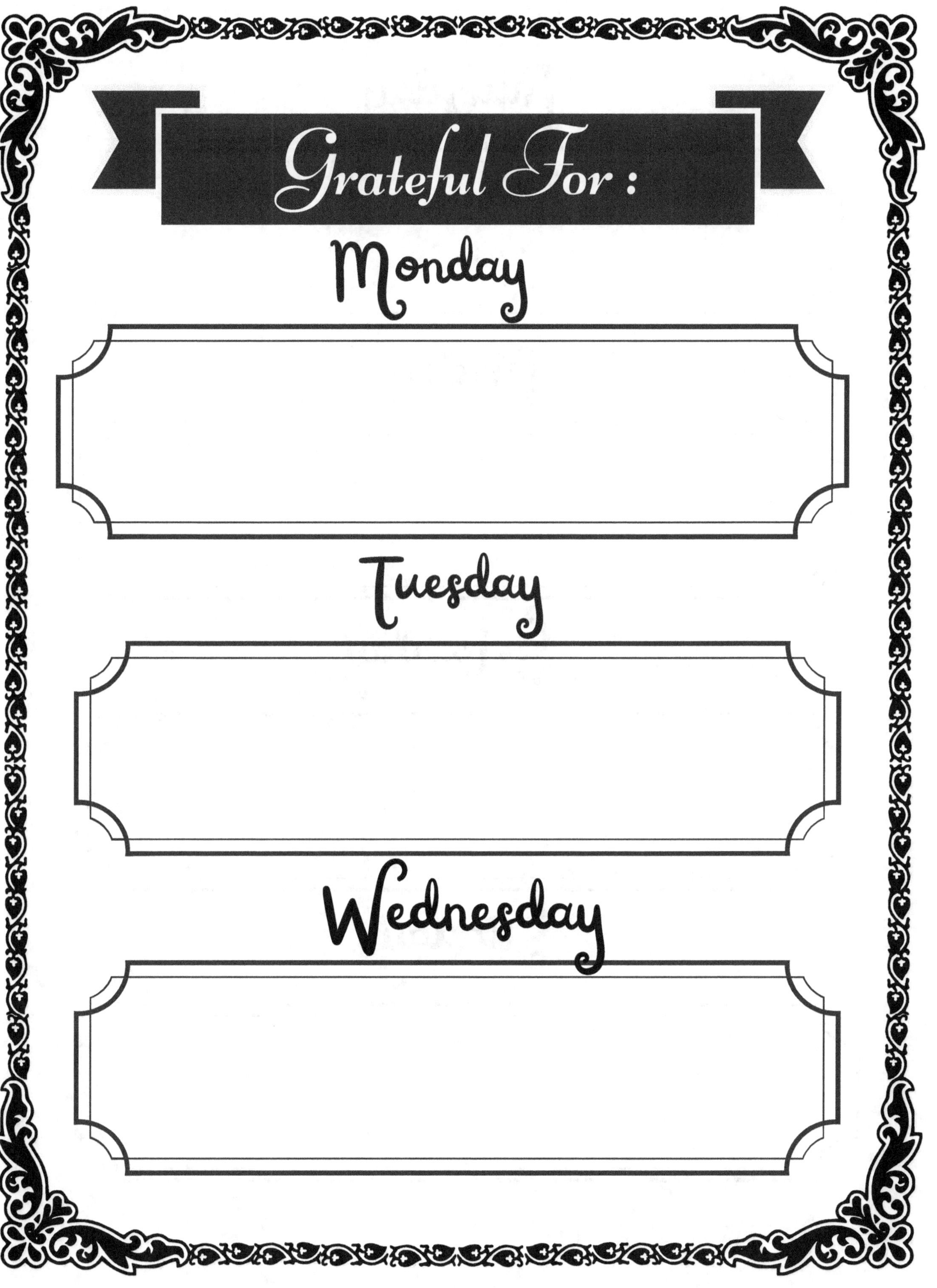

Grateful For :
Monday
Tuesday
Wednesday

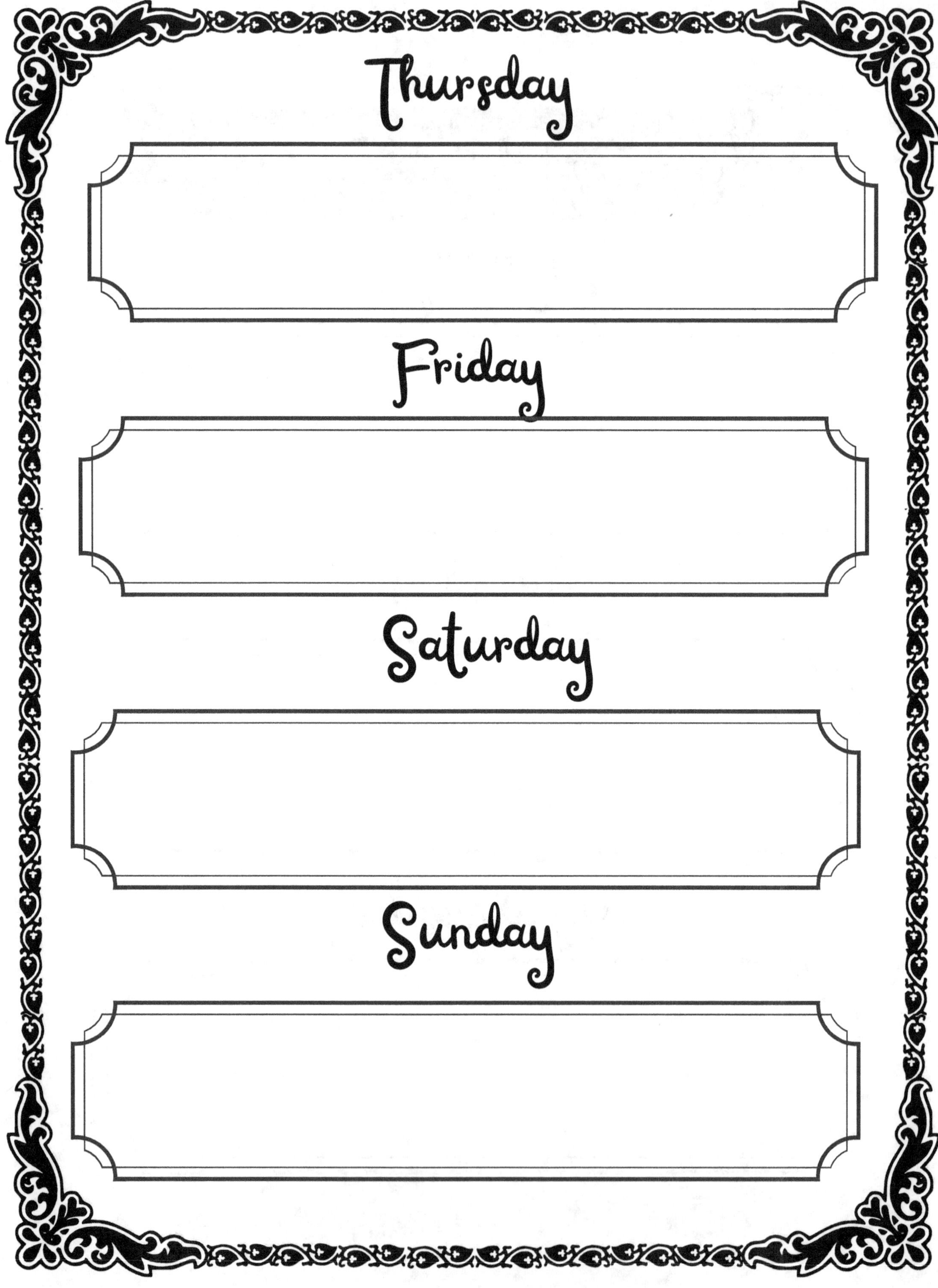

Thursday
Friday
Saturday
Sunday

Notes

My Favorite Activities Which Make Me Happy:

I'll Try to Make Them More Often through:

Why I Love My Life

Places I love To Visit

People I am Grateful For

BOOKS
I am Grateful For

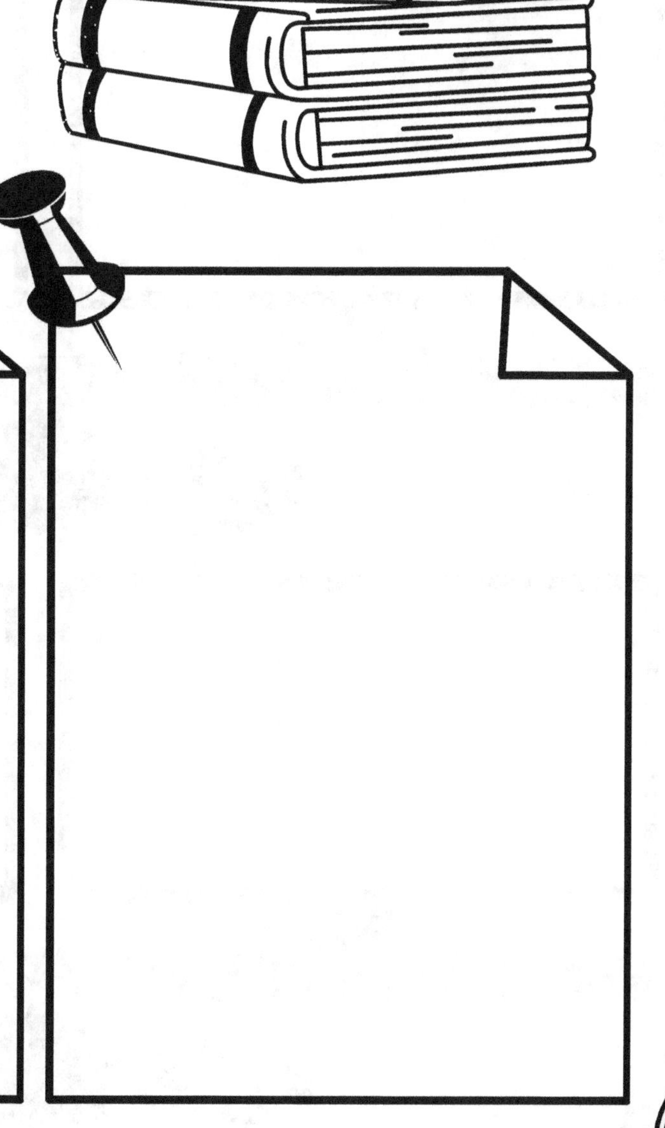

TV SHOWS

I Enjoyed Most

Dear ....
THANK YOU

Grateful For :
Monday
Tuesday
Wednesday

Thursday
Friday
Saturday
Sunday

Notes

My Favorite Activities Which Make Me Happy:

____

____

____

____

I'll Try to Make Them More Often through:

____

____

____

____

Why I Love My Life

Places I love To Visit

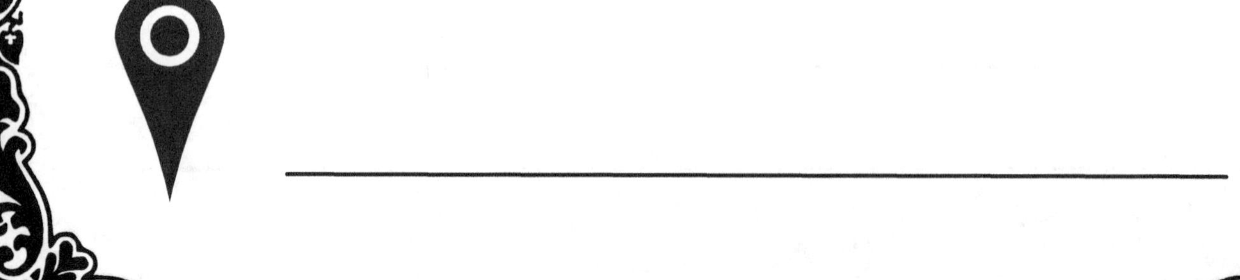

People I am Grateful For

BOOKS
I am Grateful For

GOOD BOOKS
&
GOOD COMPANY

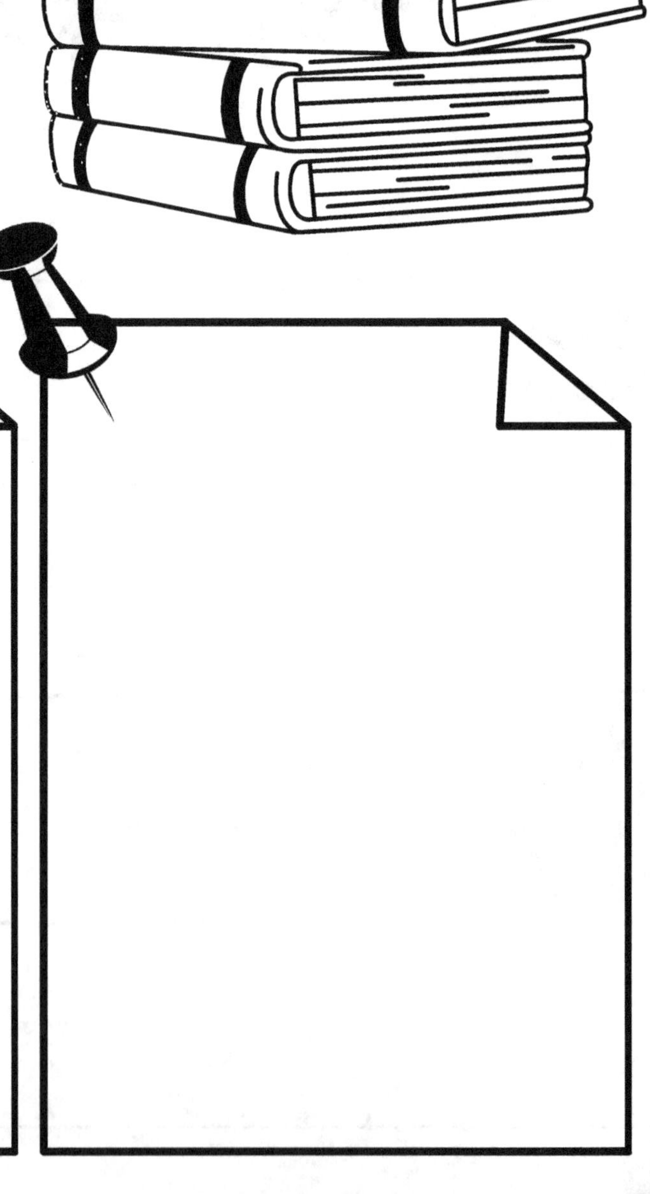

TV SHOWS
I Enjoyed Most

Dear ....

Grateful For :
Monday
Tuesday
Wednesday

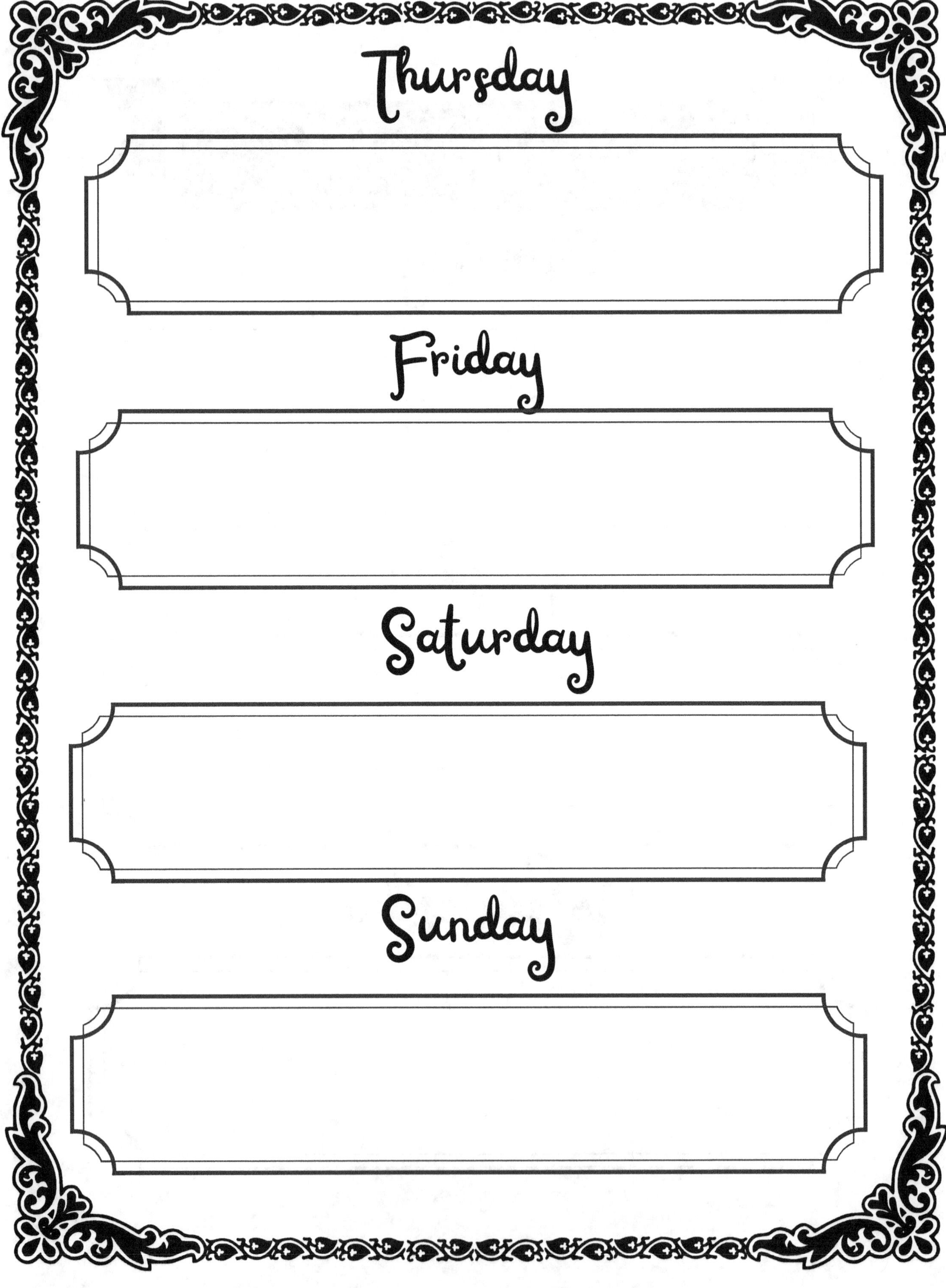
Thursday
Friday
Saturday
Sunday

Notes

My Favorite Activities Which Make Me Happy:

____

____

____

____

I'll Try to Make Them More Often through:

____

____

____

____

Why I Love My Life

Places I love To Visit

People
I am Grateful For

BOOKS
I am Grateful For

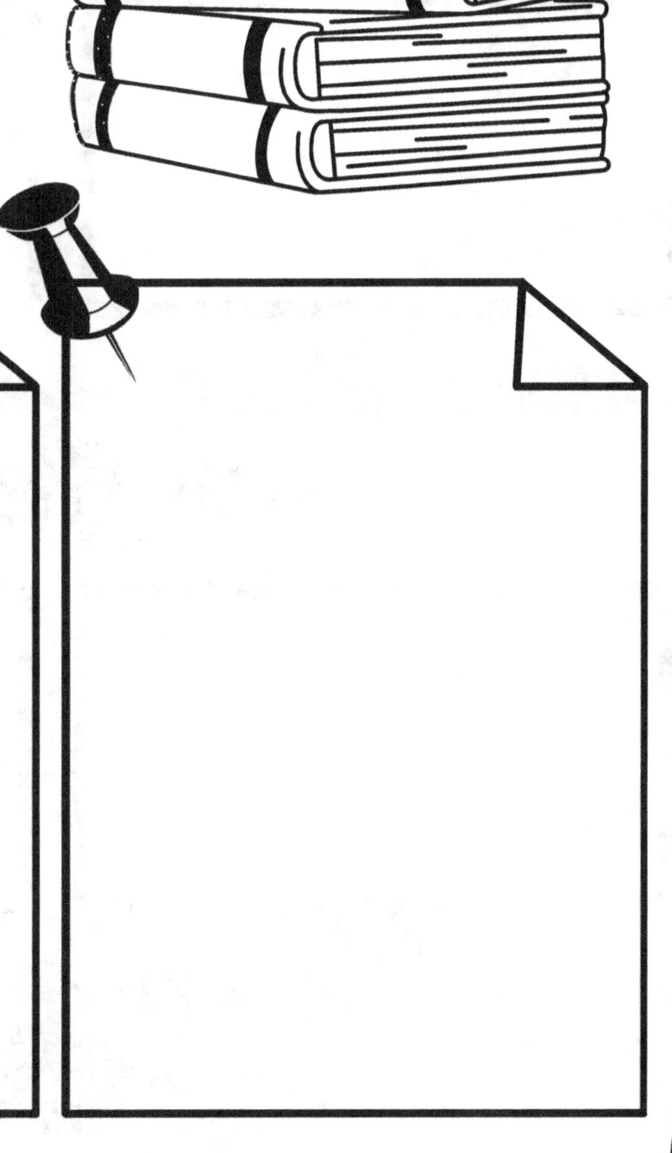

TV SHOWS
I Enjoyed Most

Dear
THANK YOU

Grateful For :
Monday
Tuesday
Wednesday

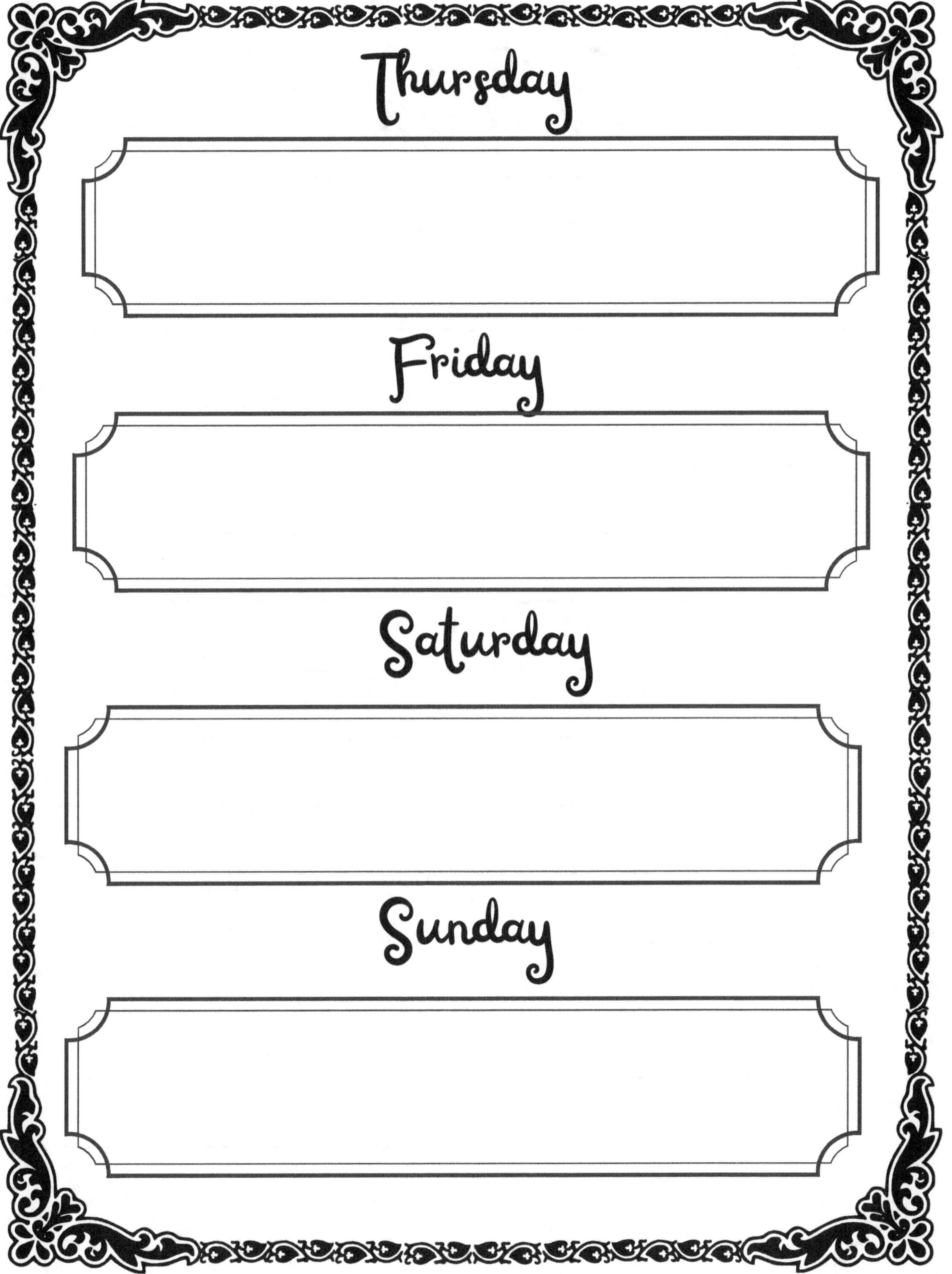

Thursday
Friday
Saturday
Sunday

Notes

Date:

My Favorite Activities Which Make Me Happy:

____

____

____

____

____

I'll Try to Make Them More Often through:

____

____

____

____

____

Why I Love My Life

Places I love To Visit

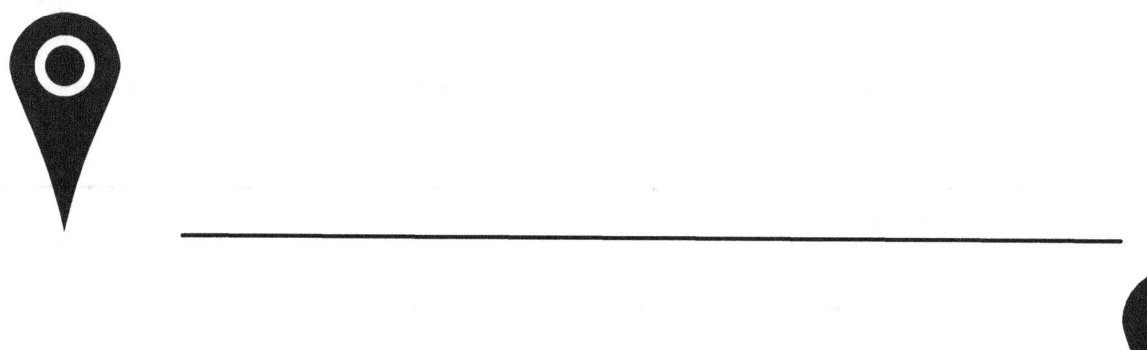

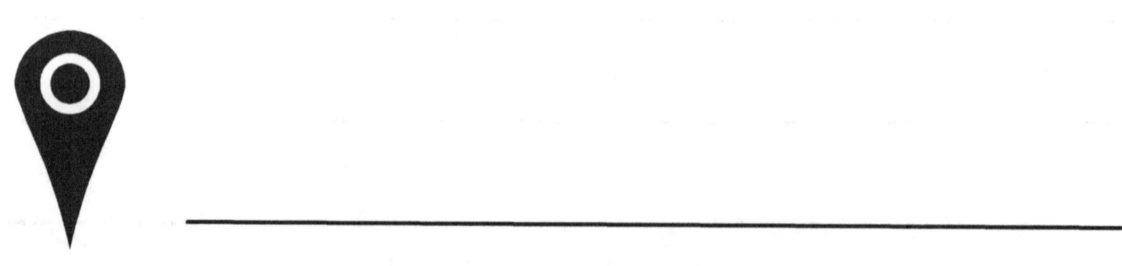

People I am Grateful For

BOOKS
I am Grateful For

GOOD BOOKS
&
GOOD COMPANY

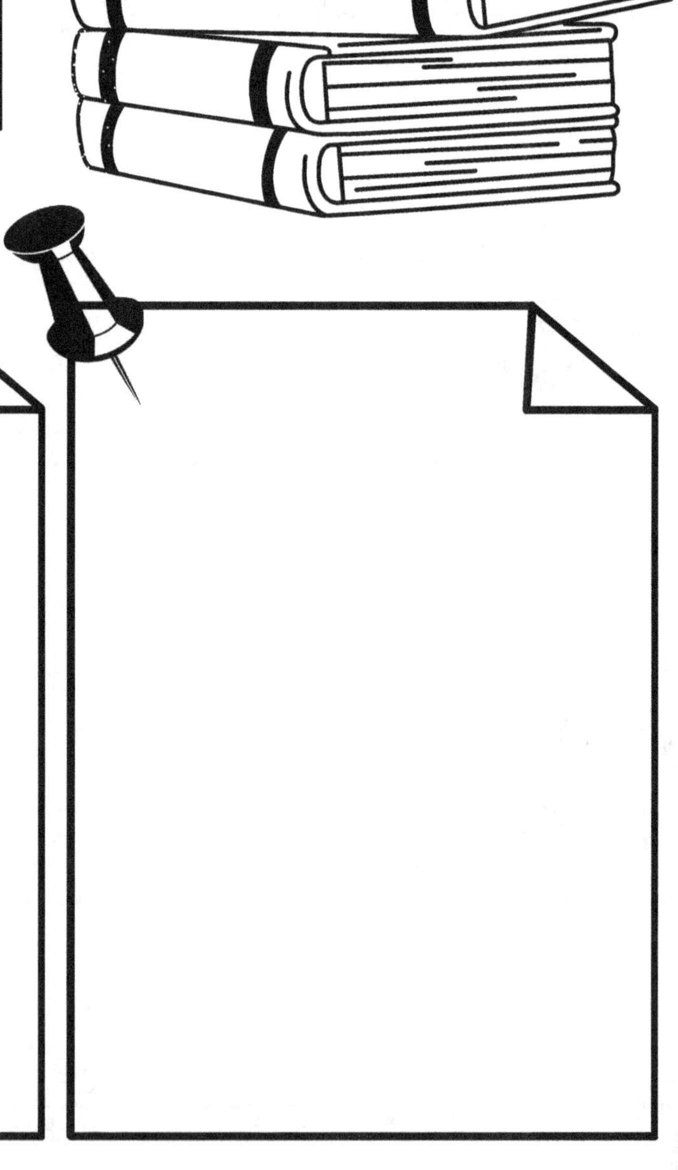

TV SHOWS
I Enjoyed Most

Dear
THANK YOU

Grateful For :
Monday
Tuesday
Wednesday

Thursday
Friday
Saturday
Sunday

Notes

My Favorite Activities Which Make Me Happy:

I'll Try to Make Them More Often through:

Why I Love My Life

Places I love To Visit

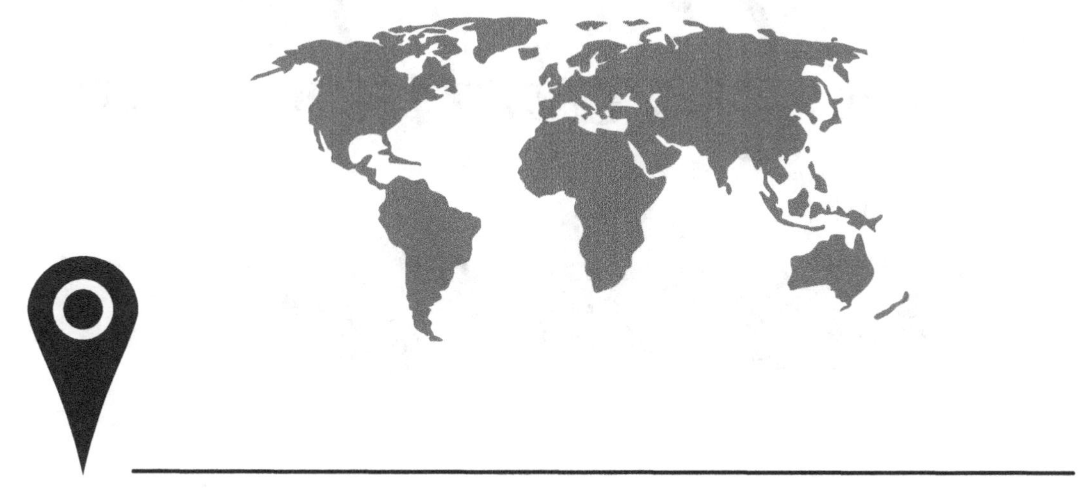

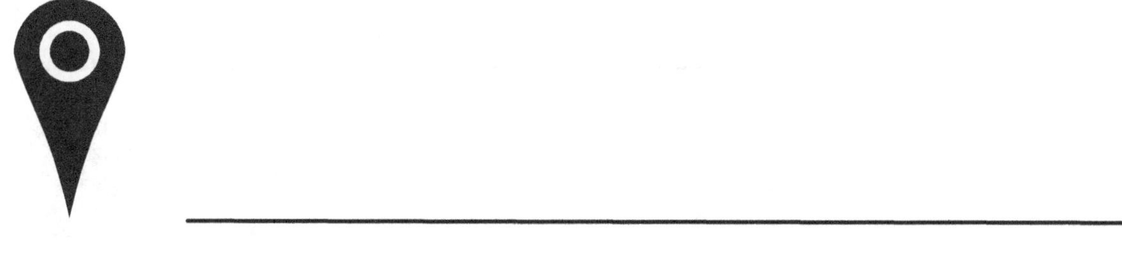

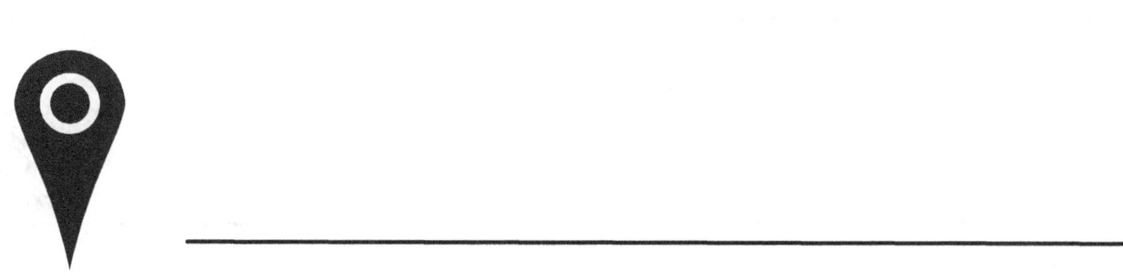

People
I am Grateful For

BOOKS

I am Grateful For

GOOD BOOKS
&
GOOD COMPANY

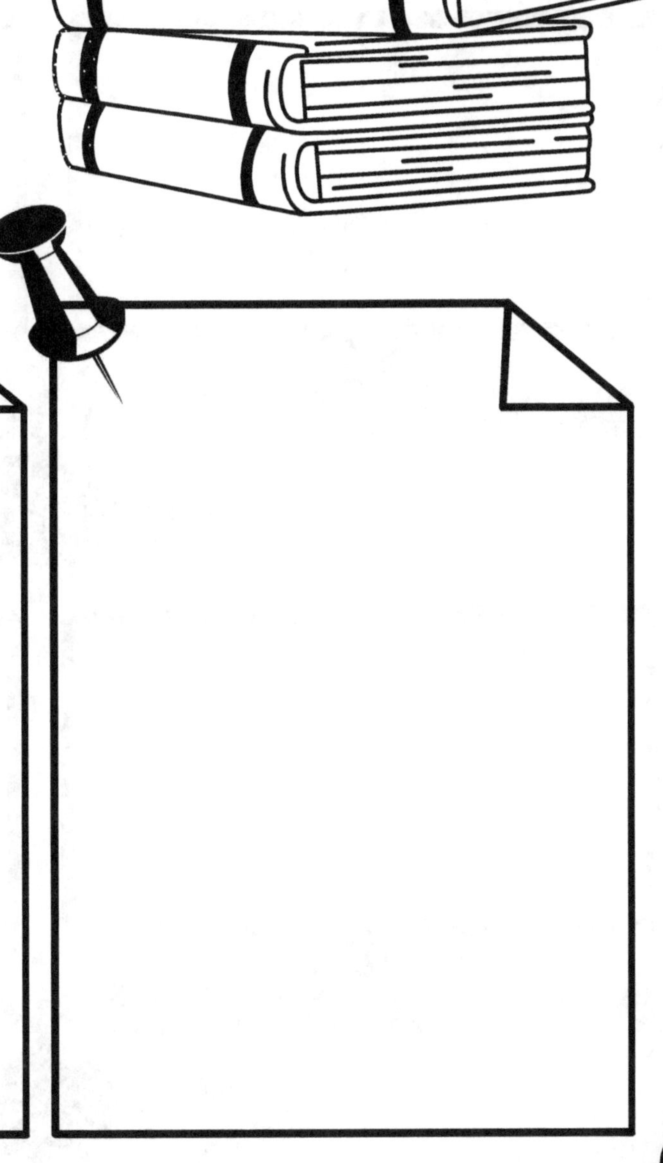

TV SHOWS
I Enjoyed Most

Dear
THANK YOU

Grateful For :
Monday
Tuesday
Wednesday

Thursday
Friday
Saturday
Sunday

Notes
Date:

My Favorite Activities Which Make Me Happy:

I'll Try to Make Them More Often through:

Why I Love My Life

Places I love To Visit

People
I am Grateful For

BOOKS
I am Grateful For

TV SHOWS
I Enjoyed Most

Dear
THANK YOU

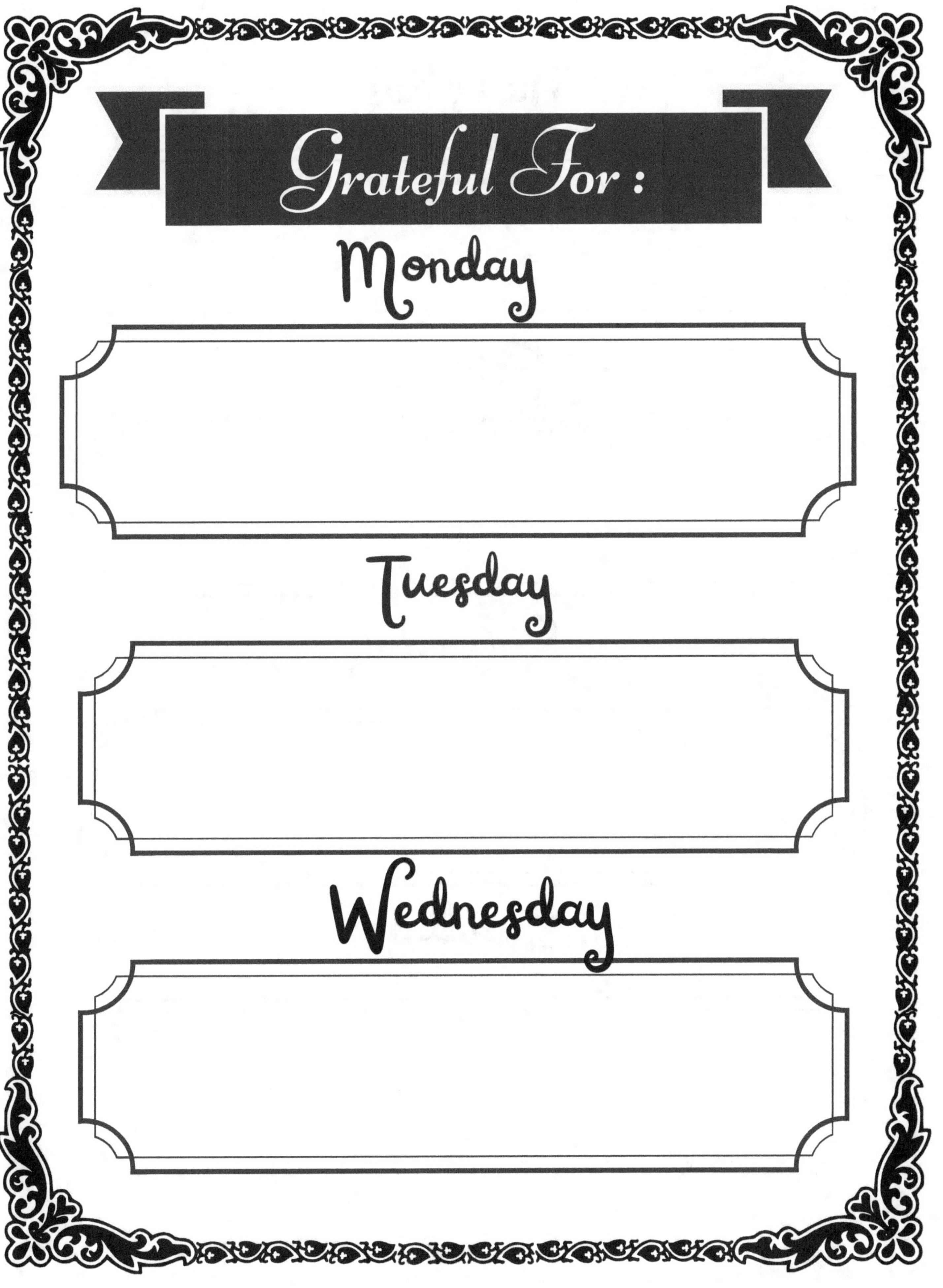

Grateful For :
Monday
Tuesday
Wednesday

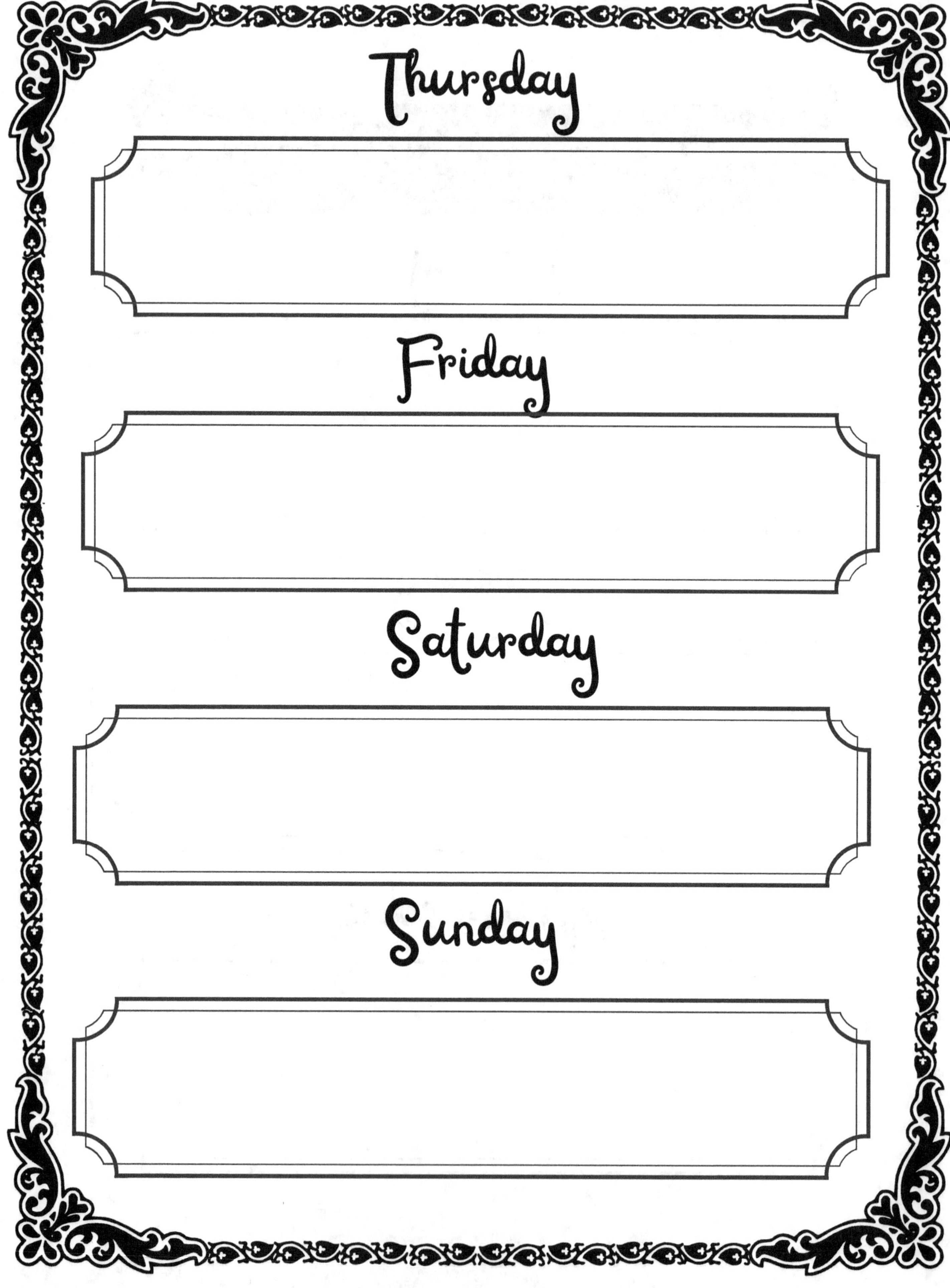

Thursday
Friday
Saturday
Sunday

Notes

My Favorite Activities Which Make
Me Happy:

I'll Try to Make Them More
Often through:

Why I Love My Life

Places I love To Visit

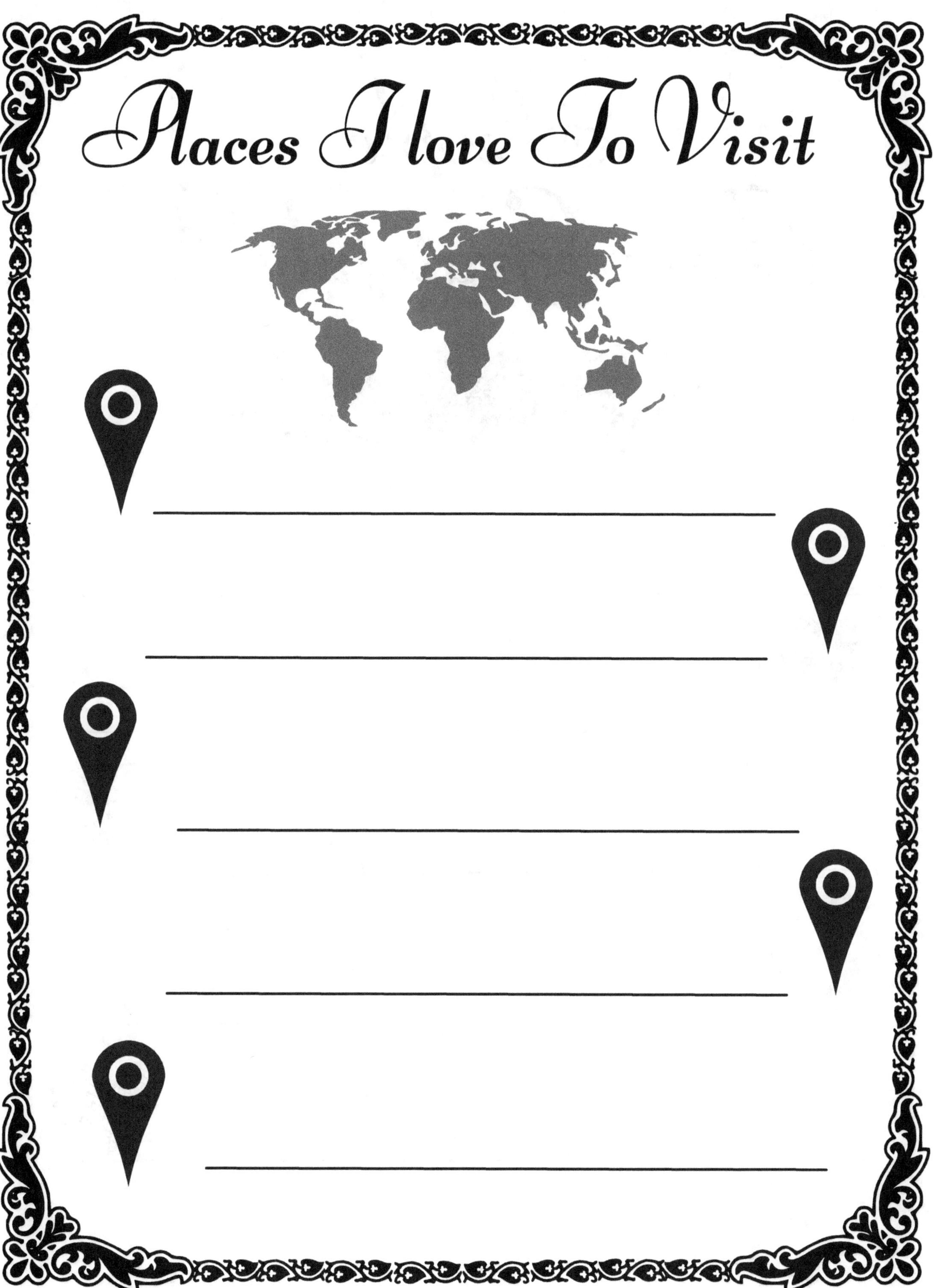

People
I am Grateful For

BOOKS
I am Grateful For

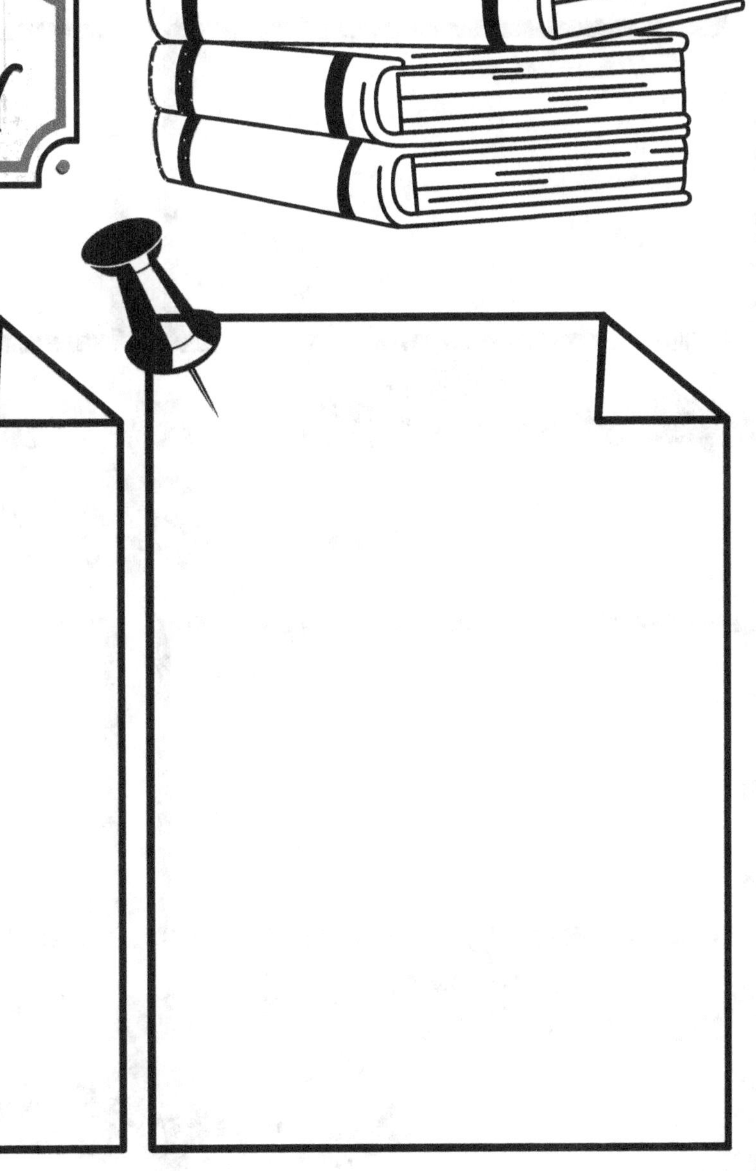

TV SHOWS
I Enjoyed Most

Dear
THANK YOU

Grateful For :
Monday
Tuesday
Wednesday

Thursday
Friday
Saturday
Sunday

Notes

My Favorite Activities Which Make Me Happy:

I'll Try to Make Them More Often through:

Why I Love My Life

Places I love To Visit

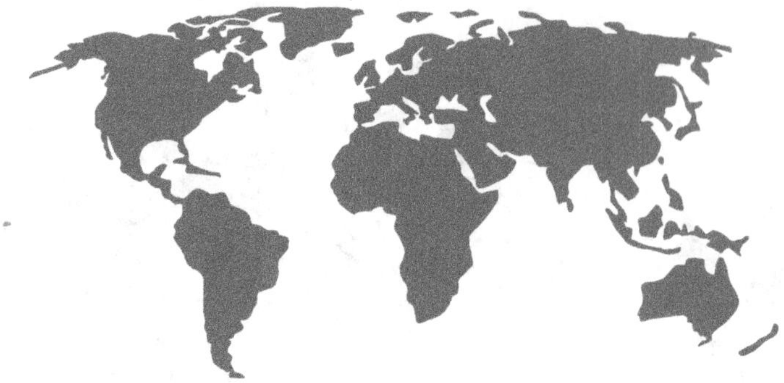

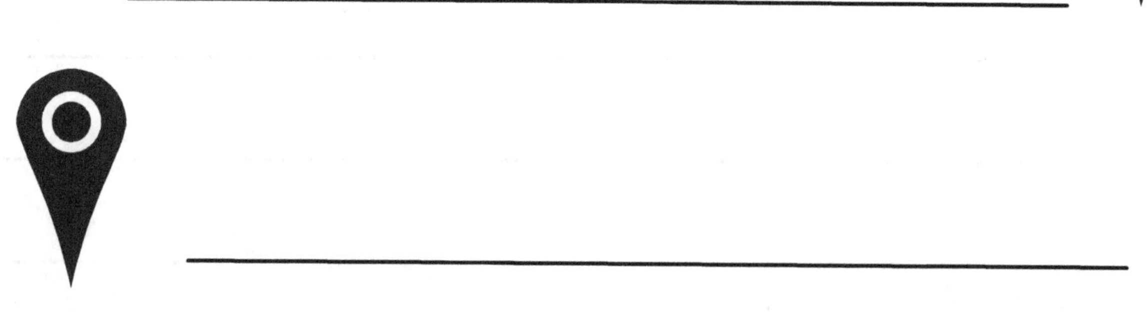

People
I am Grateful For

BOOKS
I am Grateful For

GOOD BOOKS
&
GOOD COMPANY

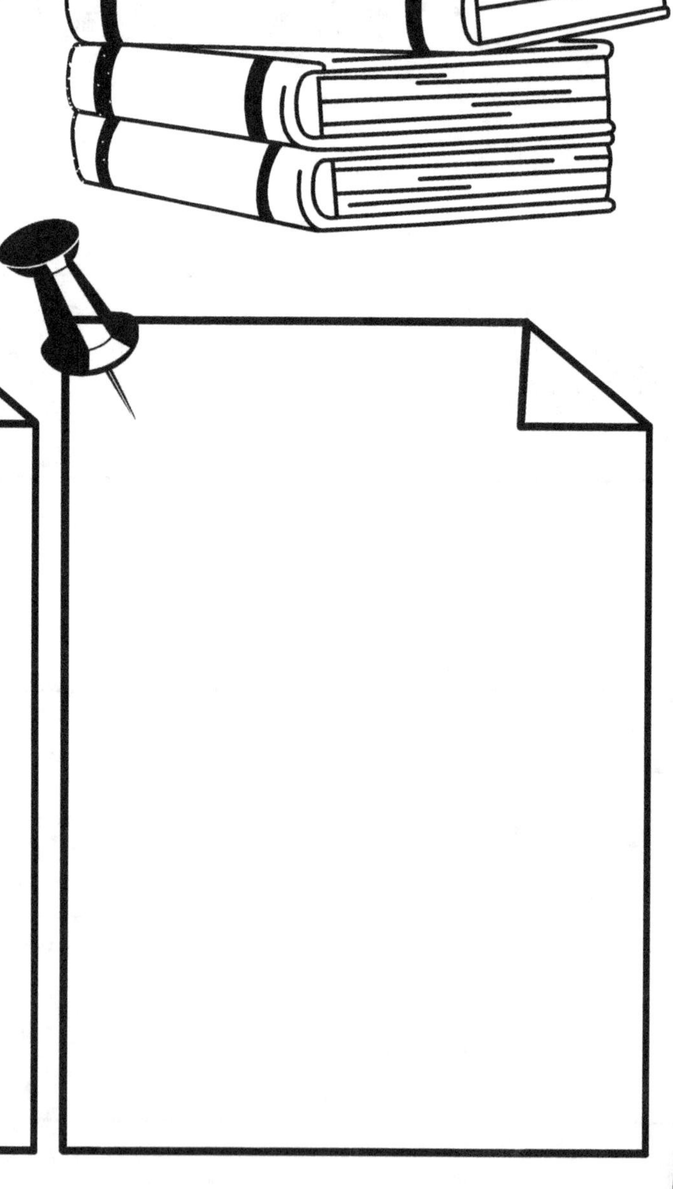

TV SHOWS
I Enjoyed Most

Dear
THANK YOU

Grateful For :
Monday
Tuesday
Wednesday

Thursday
Friday
Saturday
Sunday